WONDERS OF SINGAPORE : A PREPARATION TRAVEL GUIDE

BELLA PHILLIPS

1

TABLE OF CONTENTS

Introduction to Singapore

Singapore, often referred to as the "Lion City," is a small island nation and city-state located in Southeast Asia. It is one of the world's most prosperous and modern nations, known for its impressive economic growth, cleanliness, and cultural diversity. This introduction will provide an overview of Singapore, covering its history, geography, government, economy, culture, and more.

Geography:
Singapore is a tiny island nation situated at the southern tip of the Malay Peninsula. It covers an area of approximately 725.7 square kilometers (280.2 square miles) and is connected to the Malaysian state of Johor in the north via a causeway. The country is relatively flat, with its highest point, Bukit Timah Hill, standing at just 164 meters (538 feet) above sea level. Despite its small size, Singapore has a strategic location, making it a significant hub for trade and commerce.

History:
The history of Singapore is rich and diverse. It was originally inhabited by indigenous Malay peoples and became a trading post for the Sumatran Srivijaya Empire. In the 14th century, it was part of

the Majapahit Empire. By the 19th century, the British established a settlement on the island, which later became a major trading port of the British East India Company. It was occupied by the Japanese during World War II and gained independence from Malaysia in 1965, forming the modern nation we know today.

Government:
Singapore is a parliamentary republic with a unique political system. The government is headed by a President, who serves as the ceremonial head of state, while executive authority is vested in the Prime Minister. The dominant political party is the People's Action Party (PAP), which has been in power since independence and has played a crucial role in shaping the country's policies.

Economy:
Singapore boasts one of the world's most developed and open economies. It is renowned for its financial services, trade, and manufacturing sectors. The country is a global financial hub, home to numerous multinational corporations and banks. Its strategic location, excellent infrastructure, and pro-business policies have made it a preferred destination for foreign investments.

Culture:
Singapore's culture is a rich tapestry of influences from various ethnic groups. The major ethnic communities in Singapore include Chinese, Malay, Indian, and Eurasian. This diversity is celebrated in the form of cultural festivals, traditions, and a wide array of culinary delights. The country is known for its impeccable cleanliness and strict regulations, which contribute to its well-maintained environment.

Language:
Singapore has four official languages: English, Malay, Mandarin Chinese, and Tamil. English is widely used in education, business, and government, which facilitates communication in this multicultural society.

Tourism:
Singapore is a popular tourist destination, offering a wide range of attractions. These include iconic landmarks like the Marina Bay Sands resort, Gardens by the Bay, Sentosa Island, and the historic district of Chinatown. The city is also famous for its shopping, vibrant nightlife, and delectable street food.

Challenges:

Despite its prosperity, Singapore faces challenges such as a high cost of living, concerns about political freedoms, and the need to balance economic growth with environmental sustainability. The government's approach to these challenges has been a topic of global interest.

In conclusion, Singapore is a remarkable nation that has transformed itself from a trading post into a global economic powerhouse in a relatively short period. Its combination of cultural diversity, economic success, and disciplined governance makes it a unique and intriguing place to explore and understand.

Chapter 1.

- *Geography and Climate*

Geography:
Singapore is a small island city-state located in Southeast Asia. It is situated at the southern tip of the Malay Peninsula and is separated from Malaysia by the narrow Johor Strait. The country's geographic coordinates are approximately 1.3521° N latitude and 103.8198° E longitude. Singapore is known for its compact size, covering an area of about 725.7 square kilometers, making it one of the world's smallest countries.

Despite its limited land area, Singapore has expanded its territory through land reclamation projects, increasing its size over the years. The island's terrain is relatively flat, with its highest point, Bukit Timah Hill, reaching only 163 meters above sea level. The landscape predominantly consists of urban areas, lush greenery in parks, and some remaining pockets of natural forests and wetlands.

Climate:
Singapore experiences a tropical rainforest climate characterized by high temperatures and high

humidity throughout the year. The climate can be divided into two main monsoon seasons:

1. Northeast Monsoon (December to early March): During this period, Singapore receives more rainfall, with frequent short and heavy showers. The weather is relatively cooler, and the northeast monsoon brings wetter conditions due to the northeast winds.

2. Southwest Monsoon (June to September): This season is marked by drier and hotter weather. Rainfall is less frequent, and Singapore experiences a higher number of sunshine hours. However, occasional thunderstorms and heavy rain can occur.

Singapore's average annual temperature ranges from 24°C to 31°C (75°F to 88°F), making it a consistently warm destination. The relative humidity remains high, typically exceeding 80% throughout the year, which contributes to the island's often sticky and sultry conditions.

Singapore is prone to occasional haze, particularly during the dry months when forest fires in neighboring countries release smoke and pollutants into the atmosphere, affecting air quality. The country's position near the equator ensures that it receives fairly consistent daylight hours, with minimal variation in day length throughout the year.

Despite its small size and predictable climate, Singapore is vulnerable to the effects of climate change, such as rising sea levels and increased temperatures. The government has been actively implementing measures to address these challenges, including the construction of reservoirs, green spaces, and sustainable urban planning to mitigate flooding and enhance the quality of life in this dynamic and cosmopolitan city-state.

- *Cultural Diversity*

Cultural diversity in Singapore is a complex and dynamic phenomenon that has evolved over centuries. The city-state is often referred to as a melting pot of cultures, and this diversity is one of its most defining characteristics. Several key factors contribute to the rich tapestry of cultures in Singapore:

1. Historical Background:
   Singapore's history is marked by waves of migration and colonial influence. The indigenous Malays, Chinese, Indians, and various ethnic groups from the Malay Archipelago initially

inhabited the region. British colonial rule in the 19th and 20th centuries further shaped the cultural landscape by attracting a diverse range of immigrants.

2. Ethnic Groups:

Singapore's population is composed of several major ethnic groups, including the Chinese, Malays, Indians, and Eurasians. Each of these groups has its own unique customs, traditions, languages, and religions. The Chinese form the largest ethnic group, followed by Malays, Indians, and others.

3. Religious Diversity:

Singapore is home to various religions, including Buddhism, Islam, Hinduism, Christianity, and Taoism, among others. The government promotes religious harmony and tolerance through policies that encourage interfaith dialogue and understanding.

4. Language:

Singapore has four official languages: English, Mandarin, Malay, and Tamil. The multilingual nature of the society reflects its diverse population. English serves as the lingua franca and is used for administration and education.

5. Festivals and Celebrations:

A distinctive feature of Singapore's cultural diversity is the wide array of festivals celebrated throughout the year. Chinese New Year, Deepavali, Hari Raya Puasa, and Christmas are just a few examples. These celebrations are marked by colorful parades, religious rituals, and communal gatherings.

6. Cuisine:

Singaporean cuisine is a fusion of various culinary traditions. Hawker centers and food stalls offer dishes from Chinese, Malay, Indian, Peranakan, and other cuisines. Signature dishes like Hainanese chicken rice, laksa, and roti prata are beloved by both locals and tourists.

7. Arts and Culture:

Singapore boasts a thriving arts and culture scene. The National Museum, Peranakan Museum, and National Gallery showcase the country's diverse heritage. Local arts, music, and dance reflect the multicultural society and contribute to the preservation of traditional practices.

8. Government Policies:

The Singaporean government plays a significant role in maintaining cultural diversity. It has implemented policies that promote racial harmony, such as the Group Representation Constituency system in politics and ethnic integration in public housing.

9. National Identity:
   The concept of a "Singaporean identity" is a dynamic one, closely tied to the nation's multiculturalism. The government emphasizes shared values, such as respect for diversity and social harmony, as part of the Singaporean identity.

10. Challenges:
    While Singapore's cultural diversity is a source of strength, it can also present challenges related to maintaining harmony and addressing cultural tensions. The government's approach to these issues is carefully balanced, with policies aimed at preserving the nation's social fabric.

In conclusion, cultural diversity in Singapore is a fascinating and integral aspect of the nation's identity. It is the result of centuries of historical influences, migration, and government policies that have created a unique and harmonious multicultural society. Singapore's ability to embrace and celebrate this diversity while promoting unity serves as a model for other nations seeking to build cohesive and inclusive societies.

Chapter 2. Essential Travel Information

- *Visa and Entry Requirements*

Visa and entry requirements in Singapore can vary depending on your nationality, the purpose of your visit, and the duration of your stay.

1. Visa-Free Entry: Citizens of many countries can enter Singapore for short visits (usually up to 30 to 90 days) without a visa. The specific duration depends on your nationality. For example, U.S., EU, and Commonwealth citizens typically enjoy visa-free access.

2. Tourist Visa: If you're from a country that does not have visa-free access to Singapore, you will need to apply for a Tourist Visa, which allows you to stay for tourism purposes. This is usually for a duration of up to 30 days, but it can be extended.

3. Social Visit Pass (Short-Term): If you're visiting friends or family, attending business meetings, or seeking medical treatment in Singapore, you may apply for a Social Visit Pass (Short-Term). This typically allows a stay of up to 30 days and is extendable.

4. Business Visa: For business-related activities, you may need a Business Visa or a Social Visit Pass (Short-Term) if you are attending meetings or conferences.

5. Student Visa: If you plan to study in Singapore, you will need a Student Pass, which is typically arranged by the educational institution where you've been accepted.

6. Work Pass: To work in Singapore, you must obtain a Work Pass, such as an Employment Pass for professionals, an S Pass for mid-skilled workers, or a Work Permit for unskilled labour.

7. Long-Term Visit Pass: For family members of Employment Pass and S Pass holders, a Long-Term Visit Pass is required.

8. Permanent Residency: If you plan to live in Singapore permanently, you may consider applying for Permanent Residency (PR). The PR status allows you to live and work in Singapore without the need for a separate work pass.

9. Dependent Pass: If you are accompanying a family member who holds an Employment Pass or

S Pass, you can apply for a Dependent Pass to stay in Singapore.

10. Special Pass: In certain situations, like medical emergencies, you can apply for a Special Pass to extend your stay temporarily.

It's important to note that immigration policies and requirements can change over time, so I recommend checking the official website of the Immigration and Checkpoints Authority (ICA) of Singapore for the most up-to-date information on visa and entry requirements. Additionally, always ensure that your passport is valid for at least six months beyond your intended date of departure from Singapore and that you have the necessary supporting documents and funds for your stay.

- Currency and Money Matters

Singapore is known for its robust financial system and stable currency. The currency used in Singapore is the Singapore Dollar, abbreviated as SGD or represented by the symbol "$." Here's a comprehensive overview of currency and money matters in Singapore:

1. Currency Notes and Coins:

- Singapore's currency notes come in denominations of $2, $5, $10, $50, $100, $1,000, and $10,000. The latter two are rarely used in daily transactions.

- Coins are available in 5, 10, 20, and 50 cents, as well as $1 denominations.

2. Currency Exchange:

- Currency exchange is widely available at banks, exchange bureaus, and even at the airport. Rates may vary slightly between providers, so it's advisable to check for the best rates.

- Many ATMs in Singapore accept international cards, making it convenient for tourists to withdraw Singapore Dollars.

3. Exchange Rates:

- The exchange rate between SGD and other major currencies fluctuates and is influenced by economic factors. You can easily find the current exchange rate through financial news outlets or currency conversion websites.

4. Cash vs. Cards:

- Singapore is highly advanced in terms of cashless payments. Credit and debit cards are widely accepted at most establishments. Cash is, of course, still useful for small purchases and in places that do not accept cards.

5. ATMs and Banking:
   - Singapore has a well-developed banking infrastructure. ATMs are widely available throughout the country. You can access ATMs with foreign cards, but check if your bank charges any fees for international withdrawals.

6. Budgeting:
   - Singapore is considered one of the more expensive cities in Asia. Be prepared for higher costs, especially in terms of accommodation, dining, and entertainment.

7. Tipping and Service Charges:
   - Tipping is not a common practice in Singapore. Service charges are often included in restaurant bills, typically ranging from 10% to 15%.

8. Currency Stability:
   - The Singapore Dollar is known for its stability. The Monetary Authority of Singapore (MAS) actively manages the exchange rate to keep inflation in check and promote economic stability.

9. Currency Risks:

- While the SGD is stable, it's still essential to be aware of currency risks if you're dealing with large sums of money or investments. Fluctuations can impact the value of investments or cross-border transactions.

10. Foreign Exchange Services:
   - If you need to engage in forex trading or international money transfers, Singapore offers various financial institutions and online platforms for these purposes.

11. Legal and Regulatory Framework:
   - The Singaporean government closely regulates its financial sector, and its regulatory body, the MAS, ensures that financial institutions adhere to strict standards.

12. Emerging Technologies:
   - Singapore is also known for its innovation in the fintech sector. The country has been actively exploring the use of blockchain and cryptocurrencies in its financial system.

In summary, Singapore's currency and money matters are characterized by stability, a sophisticated financial sector, and a strong emphasis on cashless transactions. Travelers and investors will find the financial infrastructure in Singapore to be well-developed and accommodating. However, it's essential to be aware of currency exchange rates and potential fees when conducting financial transactions in the country.

- *Language and Communication*

Language and communication in Singapore are fascinating topics due to the country's multicultural and multilingual society. Singapore's linguistic landscape reflects its diverse heritage and its pursuit of a harmonious, inclusive society. In this overview, we'll explore the various languages, communication patterns, and the role of language policies in Singapore.

1. Languages in Singapore:
   - Official Languages: Singapore has four official languages: English, Mandarin Chinese, Malay, and Tamil. This choice reflects the ethnic diversity of the country's population.
   - Diverse Linguistic Groups: The population consists of various ethnic groups, including Chinese, Malay, Indian, and Eurasian communities, each bringing their languages and dialects.

2. The Role of English:

- Lingua Franca: English is the most widely used language and serves as a lingua franca for Singaporeans of different ethnic backgrounds.
- Medium of Instruction: English is the medium of instruction in schools, making it essential for education and the workplace.

3. Chinese Languages:
- Mandarin: Mandarin is taught in schools and is used as a common language for the Chinese community, despite the diversity of Chinese dialects.
- Chinese Dialects: Various Chinese dialects like Hokkien, Teochew, and Cantonese are spoken by different Chinese communities.

4. Malay and Tamil:
- Malay: Malay is the national language of Singapore and plays a crucial role in the country's identity.
- Tamil: Tamil is an official language and is primarily spoken by the Indian community.

5. Code-Switching and Bilingualism:
- Singaporeans often engage in code-switching, seamlessly transitioning between languages in conversation. This practice reflects the country's linguistic diversity.

6. Communication Styles:

   - Politeness and Respect: Singaporean communication emphasizes politeness and respect, often using honorifics and titles when addressing others.

   - Indirectness: Communication can be indirect, relying on non-verbal cues and gestures.

7. Language Policies:

   - Bilingualism Policy: The Singaporean government has promoted bilingualism, encouraging citizens to be proficient in their mother tongue and English.

   - Language Education: The education system offers a range of language courses and Mother Tongue Language (MTL) programs.

   - Speak Mandarin Campaign: An initiative to encourage the use of Mandarin among Chinese Singaporeans, promoting language harmony.

8. Challenges and Identity:

   - Singapore's language policies aim to foster a sense of national identity. However, they also face challenges in preserving heritage languages, which may be at risk of decline.

9. Media and Entertainment:

- Local media and entertainment are often produced in multiple languages to cater to the diverse population, with programs in English, Mandarin, Malay, and Tamil.

10. Language and Globalization:
   - As a global hub for business and commerce, English proficiency is a crucial asset for Singaporeans in an international context.

In conclusion, language and communication in Singapore are a reflection of its multiculturalism, shaped by language policies that aim to foster a cohesive national identity. English serves as the linchpin in this linguistic mosaic, while other languages and dialects are cherished for their cultural significance. The code-switching and bilingualism practiced by Singaporeans are testimony to their adaptability and respect for the country's linguistic diversity.

Chapter 3. Getting Around

- *Public Transportation*

Public transportation in Singapore is known for its efficiency, accessibility, and reliability. The city-state has developed a world-class public transport system that plays a crucial role in reducing traffic congestion and promoting sustainable urban development. Here's an overview of public transportation in Singapore:

1. Mass Rapid Transit (MRT):
   - The MRT system is the backbone of public transportation in Singapore, consisting of several lines that connect the city and its suburbs. There were several lines, including the North-South Line, East-West Line, Circle Line, and more.
   - MRT trains are clean, punctual, and air-conditioned, making them a popular choice for daily commuters.

2. Bus Services:
   - Singapore's extensive bus network complements the MRT system. Buses cover virtually every corner of the city and offer convenient transportation options, especially in areas not served by the MRT.

- There are several bus operators, and commuters can use contactless payment methods like the Singapore Tourist Pass or SimplyGo for seamless travel.

3. LRT (Light Rail Transit):
  - LRT lines serve specific neighbourhoods and connect them to MRT stations. The LRT system is an integral part of Singapore's public transportation, especially in residential estates.

4. Taxi and Ride-Sharing Services:
  - Singapore also has a well-regulated taxi industry. Commuters can hail taxis on the streets, use ride-sharing services like Grab, or book taxis in advance through mobile apps.

5. Fares and Payment Methods:
  - Singapore offers various fare payment options, including the contactless EZ-Link card, Singapore Tourist Pass, and SimplyGo, which allow commuters to pay for rides across different transport modes with a single card.

6. Integration and Connectivity:
  - Singapore's public transportation system is designed for seamless integration. Transfers

between MRT, bus, and LRT are straightforward, minimising travel hassles.

 - Integration also extends to connectivity with other modes of transport, such as cycling and walking. Many MRT stations have facilities for cyclists, and the city promotes pedestrian-friendly infrastructure.

7. Accessibility:
 - Singapore places a strong emphasis on making public transportation accessible to all. Most MRT stations and buses are wheelchair-friendly, and there are designated seats for the elderly and individuals with disabilities.

8. Innovation and Sustainability:
 - Singapore continually invests in technology and sustainability. The city has introduced electric buses, autonomous shuttles, and initiatives to reduce emissions and energy consumption.

9. Challenges:
 - Singapore's public transportation system is highly regarded, but it faces challenges such as overcrowding during peak hours and the need for continuous maintenance and expansion to keep up with the city's growth.

In conclusion, Singapore's public transportation system is a shining example of efficient urban planning. It provides a model for other cities aiming to reduce traffic congestion, promote sustainability, and enhance the overall quality of life for their residents and visitors.

- *Taxis and Ride-Sharing*

Taxis and ride-sharing services play a crucial role in Singapore's transportation ecosystem, providing residents and visitors with convenient, safe, and efficient ways to get around the city-state. Singapore has a well-regulated and highly organized transportation system, and both taxis and ride-sharing services are integral parts of this system. Let's delve into the details of taxis and ride-sharing in Singapore.

Taxis in Singapore:
Taxis have been a staple of Singapore's transportation system for decades. They are easily recognizable by their distinctive color – most taxis in Singapore are painted in bright yellow. Here are some key points about taxis in Singapore:

1. Types of Taxis: Singapore has several types of taxis, including standard yellow-top taxis, blue-top

taxis (typically larger and more spacious), and a premium class of taxis with top-notch amenities.

2. Regulation: Taxis in Singapore are strictly regulated by the Land Transport Authority (LTA). This ensures that drivers are properly licensed, vehicles are well-maintained, and fares are standardised.

3. Fares: Taxis in Singapore charge metered fares, and there are additional charges for various factors such as time of day, location, and peak hours. Fares are considered reasonable compared to many other global cities.

4. Booking: Taxis can be hailed on the street, or passengers can use various taxi-booking apps to request a ride. Popular taxi companies include ComfortDelGro, GrabTaxi, and Trans-Cab.

5. Taxi Stands: Singapore has numerous designated taxi stands throughout the city, making it easy for passengers to find a taxi when needed.

Ride-Sharing Services in Singapore:
Ride-sharing services like Uber and Grab arrived in Singapore in the mid-2010s, and they quickly gained popularity due to their convenience and

competitive pricing. Here's an overview of ride-sharing in Singapore:

1. Competition: Uber initially competed with Grab, a Southeast Asian ride-sharing platform. Eventually, Grab acquired Uber's Southeast Asian operations, becoming the dominant player in the region.

2. Mobile Apps: Passengers can book rides through the Grab app, which also offers additional services such as food delivery and payment solutions.

3. Regulation: Ride-sharing services in Singapore are regulated by the LTA, similar to taxis. This includes licensing requirements for drivers and adherence to safety and insurance standards.

4. Pricing: Ride-sharing services often offer competitive pricing, especially for shared rides, and they are known for transparent pricing. They sometimes introduce surge pricing during peak hours.

5. Options: In addition to standard rides, ride-sharing platforms in Singapore offer a range of options, including premium rides and shared rides, catering to various preferences and budgets.

Key Advantages of Taxis and Ride-Sharing in Singapore:

1. Convenience: Both taxis and ride-sharing services are readily available, making it easy to get around Singapore.

2. Safety: Singapore is known for its strict safety standards, ensuring that passengers are in safe hands.

3. Efficiency: These services contribute to Singapore's efficient transportation system, helping reduce congestion and pollution.

4. Payment: Cash and digital payment methods are widely accepted, making it convenient for passengers.

5. Tourism: Taxis and ride-sharing services are often the transportation method of choice for tourists exploring the city.

In conclusion, taxis and ride-sharing services have become integral to Singapore's transportation network, offering residents and tourists accessible, safe, and efficient options for getting around. The competition between taxis and ride-sharing platforms has led to improved services and better choices for passengers, ultimately contributing to the overall appeal of Singapore's public transportation system.

- *Walking and Biking*

Walking and biking in Singapore offer unique ways to explore the city-state's diverse landscapes, vibrant culture, and lush greenery. Let's delve into the various aspects of walking and biking in Singapore, including infrastructure, safety, popular routes, and the cultural significance of these activities.

Infrastructure:
Singapore boasts well-developed infrastructure for both walking and biking. The city's commitment to sustainability and urban planning has led to the creation of an extensive network of pedestrian walkways, cycling paths, and parks. The Park Connector Network (PCN) is a prime example, comprising more than 300 kilometers of dedicated cycling and walking routes, often adorned with lush greenery and scenic views.

Safety:

Safety is a top priority for pedestrians and cyclists in Singapore. The government has implemented various measures to ensure the well-being of those utilizing these modes of transportation. This includes proper signage, designated lanes, and frequent maintenance of paths. Helmets are mandatory for cyclists, and reflective clothing is encouraged for those riding at night.

Popular Walking Routes:
1. East Coast Park: This sprawling park offers a picturesque coastal walk with stunning views of the sea. It's a favourite spot for joggers, cyclists, and families enjoying picnics.

2. Southern Ridges: A series of interconnected walking trails that span the southern part of Singapore. Highlights include Henderson Waves, a distinctive wave-like bridge, and the lush canopy walk through the treetops.

3. Marina Bay Sands to Gardens by the Bay: Stroll along the waterfront promenade to enjoy breathtaking views of the city skyline and the iconic Supertree Grove.

4. Sentosa Boardwalk: This pedestrian walkway connects Sentosa Island to mainland Singapore, offering a scenic route across the water.

Popular Biking Routes:
1. East Coast Park Connector: Perfect for cyclists of all levels, this route offers a smooth, scenic ride along the coastline with multiple amenities like bike rentals and food stalls.

2. PCN Eastern Explorer Loop: A 42-kilometre loop that takes cyclists through the eastern part of Singapore, offering a mix of urban and natural landscapes.

3. Pulau Ubin: A rustic island accessible by a short ferry ride, Pulau Ubin features off-road biking trails amidst a more rural environment.

4. Coney Island Park: A natural haven with dirt tracks and boardwalks, providing an off-road biking experience with a rich variety of wildlife.

Cultural Significance:
Walking and biking are deeply ingrained in the Singaporean culture. Locals often partake in these activities not only for leisure and exercise but also for daily commuting. It's not uncommon to see

Singaporeans using bicycles to travel short distances or walking to nearby destinations. These modes of transportation foster a sense of community and environmental consciousness, aligning with Singapore's green initiatives.

In conclusion, walking and biking in Singapore are more than just recreational activities; they are integral to the city's identity and the well-being of its residents. The extensive infrastructure, safety measures, and diverse routes make it an ideal destination for those looking to explore the city on foot or on two wheels, while also contributing to a sustainable and healthy urban environment.

Chapter 4. Accommodation Options

- *Luxury Hotels*

Luxury hotels in Singapore are renowned for their opulence, world-class service, and breathtaking views. Singapore, a global hub of business and leisure, offers a range of high-end accommodations that cater to the most discerning travelers. Here's a overview of luxury hotels in Singapore:

1. The Ritz-Carlton, Millenia Singapore: This iconic hotel is known for its contemporary design and impressive art collection. It offers stunning views of Marina Bay and boasts Michelin-starred dining options.

2. Marina Bay Sands: Perhaps the most iconic hotel in Singapore, it features the world's largest rooftop infinity pool and a SkyPark with panoramic views. The integrated resort also includes a massive casino and numerous fine dining options.

3. The St. Regis Singapore: Located in the heart of the city, The St. Regis is known for its timeless elegance, personalized butler service, and luxurious suites. It's a favorite among business and leisure travelers.

4. Mandarin Oriental, Singapore: This hotel offers a harmonious blend of contemporary design and Oriental luxury. It overlooks Marina Bay and is celebrated for its award-winning spa and gourmet dining experiences.

5. Capella Singapore: Set on Sentosa Island, this luxurious retreat offers seclusion and tranquility. With its colonial architecture and lush surroundings, it's a haven for those seeking a romantic escape.

6. The Fullerton Bay Hotel: Situated along the picturesque waterfront, this boutique luxury hotel is celebrated for its stunning views of Marina Bay and the city skyline. It's a blend of modern sophistication and heritage.

7. The Raffles Hotel: An iconic historic hotel that's been meticulously restored, Raffles boasts timeless elegance and an air of colonial charm. It's famous for the Singapore Sling cocktail and its grand lobby.

8. Andaz Singapore: A contemporary luxury hotel in the heart of the city, Andaz offers stylish rooms with floor-to-ceiling windows, a rooftop bar with panoramic views, and a vibrant atmosphere.

9. Four Seasons Hotel Singapore: Located on Orchard Boulevard, this hotel offers a sense of urban resort living. It's known for its lush gardens, fine dining, and exceptional service.

10. The Warehouse Hotel: A unique luxury boutique hotel with an industrial-chic design, it's located in a historic building along the Singapore River. It's a favorite among those seeking a blend of history and modernity.

These luxury hotels in Singapore cater to various tastes and preferences, offering world-class amenities such as spas, fine dining, rooftop bars, and impeccable service. Singapore's status as a global business and tourism hub ensures that these establishments continually raise the bar for luxury and comfort, making it an ideal destination for those seeking a lavish and unforgettable experience.

- Boutique Stays

Boutique stays in Singapore offer travelers a unique and personalized accommodation experience in the heart of this vibrant city-state. These establishments cater to guests seeking more than just a place to sleep; they aim to provide an intimate, stylish, and often luxurious stay that

reflects the character and culture of Singapore.
Here is an overview of boutique stays in Singapore:

1. Intimate Atmosphere: Boutique stays are known
for their intimate atmosphere. These
establishments are typically smaller in scale
compared to large hotel chains, which means they
can offer more personalized and attentive service.
Guests can expect a warm and welcoming
environment where their individual needs are
prioritized.

2. Unique Design and Decor: The design and decor
of boutique stays in Singapore often showcase a
distinctive blend of modernity and local cultural
influences. Many boutique hotels and guesthouses
are housed in heritage buildings, offering a glimpse
into the city's rich history. From
Peranakan-inspired interiors to contemporary
minimalism, each establishment has a unique
character.

3. Personalised Service: Guests can look forward to
a high level of personalized service. Staff in
boutique stays tend to go the extra mile to ensure
guests have a memorable stay. This includes
tailored recommendations for dining, local

attractions, and assistance with any special requests.

4. Prime Locations: Boutique stays in Singapore are often strategically located in key areas of the city, allowing guests easy access to attractions, shopping districts, and transportation hubs. Some can be found in charming historic neighborhoods like Chinatown, Little India, or Tiong Bahru.

5. Culinary Experiences: Many boutique stays offer exceptional dining experiences. On-site restaurants and cafes often emphasize locally inspired cuisine, providing guests with a taste of Singapore's diverse culinary scene. Some may even offer cooking classes or food tours.

6. Luxury and Comfort: Although boutique stays may be smaller than traditional hotels, they do not compromise on luxury and comfort. High-quality linens, spa facilities, and well-appointed rooms are common features.

7. Cultural and Artistic Touch: Some boutique stays in Singapore actively promote local arts and culture. They may host art exhibitions, cultural performances, or even offer art-related amenities within the property.

8. Hidden Gems: Boutique stays are often considered hidden gems in the hospitality industry. They provide an exclusive experience away from the hustle and bustle of larger chain hotels. Their unique charm and character make them particularly appealing to travellers seeking something out of the ordinary.

9. Environmental Responsibility: Many boutique stays in Singapore are committed to sustainable and eco-friendly practices. They may incorporate green initiatives like energy-efficient systems and waste reduction programs.

10. Variety of Options: Singapore offers a diverse range of boutique stays, from luxury boutique hotels to cosy bed and breakfasts. This means travelers have a variety of options to choose from based on their preferences and budget.

In conclusion, boutique stays in Singapore offer travelers a distinctive and personalized experience in a city known for its cosmopolitan appeal. These establishments combine luxury, culture, and intimate service to create memorable stays that reflect the essence of this dynamic metropolis. Whether you're a tourist looking to explore

Singapore or a local seeking a staycation, boutique accommodations provide an attractive alternative to traditional hotels.

- *Budget Hostels*

Budget hostels in Singapore provide affordable accommodation options for travelers looking to explore this vibrant city without breaking the bank. Here, we'll discuss various aspects of budget hostels in Singapore.

1. Affordability:
   Budget hostels in Singapore are known for their cost-effectiveness. They offer dormitory-style rooms with multiple beds, making it possible to save on accommodation costs, which is particularly important in a city known for its high cost of living.

2. Dormitory Rooms:
   Most budget hostels primarily offer dormitory-style rooms with bunk beds. These rooms are shared with other travelers, providing a communal atmosphere where you can meet fellow globetrotters. Private rooms might also be available, but they are generally more expensive.

3. Basic Amenities:

Budget hostels typically offer basic amenities like shared bathrooms, free Wi-Fi, lockers, and communal areas where guests can socialize, cook, or relax. While the facilities may not be luxurious, they are functional and cater to the needs of budget-conscious travelers.

4. Locations:

Budget hostels can be found in various parts of Singapore, from the bustling city center to quieter suburban neighborhoods. The location of the hostel can significantly impact your access to public transportation, nearby attractions, and overall convenience.

5. Cleanliness and Safety:

Reputable budget hostels prioritize cleanliness and guest safety. Clean common areas, beds, and bathrooms are standard. Hostels often have security measures in place, such as key card access, lockers, and 24-hour reception, to ensure the safety of guests.

6. Social Atmosphere:

Budget hostels are known for their social atmosphere. They often organize events, tours, and activities that allow guests to interact with one another and explore the city together. This can be particularly appealing for solo travelers looking to make new friends.

7. Booking Options:
   Booking a bed in a budget hostel is usually done online through various booking platforms. Prices can vary depending on the time of year, so booking in advance is recommended, especially during peak travel seasons.

8. Reviews and Recommendations:
   Before choosing a budget hostel, it's a good idea to read reviews and recommendations from fellow travelers. This can help you gauge the quality of the hostel and its suitability for your needs.

9. Long-term Stays:
   Some budget hostels also accommodate long-term travelers with discounted rates. These are often digital nomads or students who want an extended stay while exploring Singapore.

10. Cultural Experience:
   Staying in a budget hostel can be a unique cultural experience. You'll meet people from all around the world, providing insights into different cultures and travel experiences.

In conclusion, budget hostels in Singapore offer an affordable and social way to explore this diverse and exciting city. While they may lack the luxury of upscale hotels, they provide a budget-friendly and community-oriented environment for travelers looking to make the most of their Singaporean adventure.

Chapter 5. Top Tourist Attractions

- *Marina Bay Sands*

Marina Bay Sands is an iconic integrated resort located in Singapore, known for its distinctive architectural design and a wide range of entertainment, hospitality, and leisure offerings. Here's an overview of this renowned landmark:

1. Architecture and Design:
   - Marina Bay Sands is instantly recognizable by its unique design, featuring three soaring towers topped by a massive sky park.
   - The resort's rooftop boasts a 340-meter-long infinity pool, which offers breathtaking views of the city skyline.

2. Accommodation:
   - The resort offers over 2,500 luxurious hotel rooms and suites, making it one of the largest hotels in Asia.
   - The rooms are well-appointed, offering modern amenities and incredible city or bay views.

3. Entertainment:
   - Marina Bay Sands is home to a plethora of entertainment options, including a world-class

casino, offering various table games and slot machines.

- The resort is known for hosting international acts and performances at the Sands Theatre and the Sands Expo and Convention Centre.

4. Shopping and Dining:
- The Shoppes at Marina Bay Sands is a high-end shopping mall featuring a wide range of designer boutiques and luxury brands.
- The resort boasts a diverse selection of dining options, from celebrity chef restaurants to local and international cuisine.

5. SkyPark:
- The SkyPark, perched atop the towers, is a major attraction. It includes lush gardens, observation decks, and the iconic infinity pool.
- It offers stunning panoramic views of the city and is a great place for relaxation and photography.

6. ArtScience Museum:
- The ArtScience Museum at Marina Bay Sands is a one-of-a-kind institution dedicated to exploring the intersection of art, science, culture, and technology.
- It features a range of interactive exhibitions and installations.

7. Convention and Exhibition Space:
   - The Sands Expo and Convention Centre provides state-of-the-art facilities for conferences, exhibitions, and events, making it a prominent business and MICE (Meetings, Incentives, Conventions, and Exhibitions) destination.

8. Sustainability:
   - Marina Bay Sands has taken steps to reduce its environmental impact, implementing various sustainability initiatives, including energy-efficient design and green building practices.

9. Location:
   - The resort is strategically situated in the heart of Singapore's financial district, with easy access to popular tourist attractions like Gardens by the Bay, the Singapore Flyer, and the Merlion Park.

10. Cultural Significance:
   - Marina Bay Sands has become an iconic symbol of modern Singapore and a key player in the city's tourism industry.
   - It has featured prominently in numerous movies and television shows, further enhancing its global recognition.

11. Events and Celebrations:
   - The resort is known for its extravagant New Year's Eve celebrations, with a grand fireworks display over the bay.
   - It also hosts various other events and celebrations throughout the year.

Marina Bay Sands has played a pivotal role in transforming Singapore's tourism landscape, offering a blend of luxury, entertainment, and culture. It continues to draw visitors from around the world, contributing to the city's reputation as a top global destination.

- Sentosa Island

Sentosa Island is a popular resort destination located in Singapore, known for its stunning beaches, world-class attractions, and vibrant entertainment options. It's a premier vacation spot that caters to a wide range of tourists, from families to adventure seekers, offering a diverse array of experiences. Let's delve into the aspects of Sentosa Island:

1. Location and Access:
Sentosa Island is situated just off the southern coast of mainland Singapore and is accessible via road, cable car, monorail, or even on foot through a

pedestrian causeway. The ease of access makes it a convenient location for both locals and tourists.

2. Beaches:
Sentosa boasts several beautiful beaches, including Palawan Beach, Siloso Beach, and Tanjong Beach. These sandy shores provide a perfect backdrop for relaxation, sunbathing, and water sports. Sentosa's beaches are well-maintained and offer a range of facilities.

3. Attractions:
Sentosa is home to a plethora of attractions, catering to various interests. Some of the most notable ones include:

  - Universal Studios Singapore: This world-renowned theme park features a variety of themed zones with thrilling rides and entertainment.

  - S.E.A. Aquarium: One of the world's largest aquariums, it showcases a diverse collection of marine life.

  - Adventure Cove Waterpark: A waterpark offering thrilling slides, wave pools, and opportunities for snorkeling with marine creatures.

- Madame Tussauds Singapore: Visitors can rub shoulders with lifelike wax figures of famous personalities from around the world.

- Wings of Time: A mesmerizing multimedia night show that combines water, laser, and fire effects to tell a captivating story.

4. Wildlife and Nature:
Sentosa is not just about attractions; it also has its fair share of natural beauty. Butterfly Park and Insect Kingdom offer an immersive experience with various species of butterflies and insects. Sentosa Nature Discovery is an informative center that showcases the island's flora and fauna.

5. Dining and Shopping:
The island offers an array of dining options, from beachfront restaurants to upscale dining establishments. Shopping enthusiasts can explore VivoCity, a massive shopping mall that's conveniently connected to Sentosa. Resorts World Sentosa also features numerous shops and boutiques.

6. Accommodation:

Sentosa offers a range of accommodation options, from luxury resorts to more budget-friendly choices, making it an ideal destination for a variety of travelers.

7. Entertainment and Events:
Throughout the year, Sentosa hosts various events and entertainment shows, including music concerts, art exhibitions, and cultural festivals, providing visitors with a dynamic and vibrant atmosphere.

8. History and Heritage:
Sentosa Island has a rich history, once known as "Pulau Blakang Mati," which means the "Island of Death from Behind" in Malay. It was historically a military fortress. Today, remnants of its military past can be explored at Fort Siloso, which has been preserved as a historical site.

In summary, Sentosa Island in Singapore is a multifaceted destination that seamlessly blends natural beauty, entertainment, and leisure. Its strategic location, a stone's throw away from the bustling city center of Singapore, makes it a must-visit location for tourists seeking a diverse and immersive vacation experience. Whether you're looking for a day of adventure, relaxation on pristine beaches, or world-class entertainment, Sentosa Island offers it all.

- *Gardens by the Bay*

Gardens by the Bay is a remarkable horticultural and architectural wonder located in Singapore. This iconic attraction, spanning 101 hectares in the heart of the city, is a testament to the city-state's commitment to creating a sustainable and green urban environment. Here's an overview of Gardens by the Bay:

1. Inception and Development:
Gardens by the Bay was officially opened in 2012, with its origins dating back to Singapore's desire to transform its image from a concrete jungle into a "City in a Garden." The government aimed to provide a green sanctuary for residents and visitors, and this project was a key part of that vision.

2. The Supertree Grove:
The Supertree Grove is arguably the most recognizable feature of Gardens by the Bay. These towering tree-like structures, ranging from 25 to 50 meters in height, are not only visually stunning but also serve practical functions. They are fitted with photovoltaic cells to harness solar energy and are used for vertical gardens. A skywalk connecting two

of the Supertrees provides breathtaking panoramic views of the gardens and the city skyline.

3. Flower Dome and Cloud Forest:
Within the Gardens, you'll find two colossal glass conservatories – the Flower Dome and the Cloud Forest. The Flower Dome replicates various Mediterranean climates and houses a wide variety of plants and flowers. The Cloud Forest, on the other hand, features a misty mountain environment with a captivating indoor waterfall. Both conservatories showcase diverse flora from around the world.

4. Outdoor Gardens:
Beyond the iconic structures, the outdoor gardens are divided into themed areas, such as the Heritage Gardens, World of Palms, and the Serene Garden. Each garden showcases different plant species and design elements, making it a rich educational experience for visitors.

5. Sustainability Initiatives:
Gardens by the Bay is not just about aesthetics; it's also a model for sustainability. It employs advanced water recycling systems, solar power generation, and rainwater harvesting to reduce its environmental impact. It serves as an educational

platform, promoting awareness of ecological issues and sustainable practices.

6. Events and Programs:
The gardens host a wide array of events, from concerts and exhibitions to fitness classes and children's programs. The annual Orchid Extravaganza and Sakura Matsuri are particularly popular. The venue is versatile, offering spaces for weddings, corporate events, and more.

7. Nighttime Spectacular:
Visiting Gardens by the Bay at night is an enchanting experience. The Supertrees come alive with a light and music show called the Garden Rhapsody. The entire garden is illuminated, creating a magical atmosphere.

8. Accessibility and Sustainability:
Gardens by the Bay is easily accessible by public transport, and the connected Marina Bay Sands resort provides additional amenities and entertainment options. Its commitment to sustainability extends to its educational programs, ensuring that visitors leave with a deeper appreciation for the environment.

Gardens by the Bay in Singapore is a testament to human ingenuity, fusing nature and technology to create a lush green oasis in the heart of a bustling metropolis. It's a symbol of Singapore's dedication to sustainable urban development and offers a refreshing and educational experience for everyone who visits.

- Chinatown

Chinatown in Singapore is a vibrant and historically rich district that has become one of the city-state's most iconic neighbourhoods. Here is an verview of Chinatown, covering its history, cultural significance, attractions, and more.

Historical Background:
Chinatown's history dates back to the early 19th century when Chinese immigrants flocked to Singapore in search of better opportunities. Over time, they established their community, which eventually became known as Chinatown. It played a crucial role in the development of the city and Singapore's identity as a multicultural society.

Cultural Significance:
Chinatown remains an important cultural enclave. It's a testament to the Chinese heritage in Singapore and serves as a living museum of sorts,

preserving traditions, customs, and culinary delights that have been passed down through generations. The vibrant Chinese New Year celebrations in Chinatown are a testament to the cultural significance of the district.

Architectural Charm:
Chinatown's unique architectural charm adds to its allure. The district is characterized by rows of colourful shophouses with intricate facades, red lanterns, and ornate designs. The Chinatown Heritage Centre, a museum in a restored shophouse, provides a glimpse into the living conditions of early Chinese immigrants.

Shopping and Dining:
Chinatown is a shopper's paradise. The streets are lined with stalls and shops selling a wide variety of goods, including traditional Chinese clothing, jewelry, antiques, and souvenirs. Food enthusiasts can explore the bustling hawker centers, street food stalls, and local restaurants serving delectable Chinese cuisine.

Religious Diversity:
Chinatown is home to several religious landmarks, including the Buddha Tooth Relic Temple and Museum, Thian Hock Keng Temple, and Sri

Mariamman Temple. These places of worship reflect the religious diversity within the Chinese community and serve as important cultural and historical sites.

Festivals and Events:
Chinatown hosts numerous festivals and events throughout the year. The Chinese New Year celebrations are a highlight, with street decorations, performances, and a lively atmosphere. Other festivals, such as the Mid-Autumn Festival and Lantern Festival, are also celebrated with gusto.

Markets and Street Vendors:
Chinatown is famous for its street markets, where you can find a wide range of products at affordable prices. The Chinatown Street Market, Smith Street Market, and Chinatown Complex Market are popular spots for bargain hunters.

Chinatown's Modern Face:
While Chinatown proudly preserves its heritage, it has also adapted to modern times. It is now home to co-working spaces, trendy bars, and boutique hotels, making it a diverse and dynamic neighbourhood.

In conclusion, Chinatown in Singapore is a captivating blend of history, culture, and modernity. It remains a must-visit destination for tourists and a cherished cultural hub for the local Chinese community. Its vibrant streets, historic sites, and culinary delights make it a place where the past and present coexist in perfect harmony.

- *Little India*

Little India is a vibrant and culturally rich neighborhood located in the heart of Singapore. It's one of the city-state's most iconic cultural enclaves, known for its deep-rooted South Asian heritage and unique atmosphere. Here's an overview of Little India in Singapore:

1. Historical Significance: Little India's history dates back to the early 19th century when Indian immigrants, mainly from the Tamil Nadu region, started settling in this area. They were drawn to Singapore for economic opportunities and played a crucial role in the development of the city.

2. Cultural Diversity: Little India is a microcosm of Indian culture in Singapore. It is a melting pot of various Indian ethnic groups, including Tamils, Punjabis, Bengalis, and Malayalees. This diversity is

reflected in the languages spoken, religious practices, and food.

3. Geographical Location: Little India is conveniently situated just north of the Singapore River, making it easily accessible from various parts of the city. The neighborhood is centered around Serangoon Road and its adjacent streets.

4. Architectural Charm: The streets of Little India are lined with colorful, ornate buildings that are reminiscent of traditional Indian architecture. Temples, mosques, and churches are interspersed throughout, adding to the cultural diversity.

5. Sri Veeramakaliamman Temple: One of the most iconic landmarks in Little India, this temple is dedicated to the Hindu goddess Kali. Its stunning architecture and intricate sculptures make it a must-visit attraction.

6. Shopping: Little India is a shopper's paradise. You can find an array of shops selling saris, spices, jewellery, and traditional Indian garments. Mustafa Centre, a massive 24/7 department store, is a prominent shopping destination in the area.

7. Dining Experience: The neighbourhood is renowned for its authentic Indian cuisine. From street food stalls to fine-dining restaurants, Little India offers a wide range of culinary experiences. Try popular dishes like biryani, dosa, and various curries.

8. Festivals and Celebrations: Little India comes alive during Indian festivals, such as Deepavali (Diwali) and Pongal. The streets are adorned with colorful decorations and lights, and cultural performances take place during these celebrations.

9. Culture and Arts: The area hosts various cultural events, including traditional dance performances, music shows, and art exhibitions. These events provide insight into the rich Indian culture and heritage.

10. Community Spirit: Little India has a close-knit community. Various associations and organisations work to preserve and promote Indian culture in Singapore. These groups often organise events and activities for both residents and visitors.

11. Transport Links: The neighbourhood is well-connected via public transport, with the Little India MRT station serving as a major

transportation hub. This makes it easy for tourists to explore the area and for residents to commute.

12. Blend of Old and New: While preserving its cultural heritage, Little India has also embraced modernity. You'll find contemporary art galleries, boutiques, and cafes alongside traditional businesses.

In conclusion, Little India in Singapore is a remarkable neighborhood that offers a captivating blend of tradition, culture, and diversity. It's a testament to the contributions of the Indian community to Singapore's history and continues to be a vibrant and essential part of the city's cultural tapestry. Whether you're interested in exploring heritage, savoring Indian cuisine, or simply immersing yourself in a unique atmosphere, Little India has something to offer to everyone.

Chapter 6. Culinary Delights

- *Local Hawker Centers*

Hawker centers in Singapore are integral to the country's culinary culture and are a cornerstone of its food scene. These local dining establishments are known for serving up an incredible variety of affordable, delicious, and diverse dishes, representing a melting pot of cultures. Here's a look at local hawker centers in Singapore:

1. Historical Context:
   Hawker centers in Singapore have a rich history that dates back to the 1950s and 1960s when the government established them as a way to regulate street food vending. Over time, these centers have evolved into clean, organized, and hygienic food courts.

2. Iconic Hawker Centers:
   - Maxwell Food Centre: Located in the heart of Chinatown, this center is renowned for dishes like Hainanese chicken rice, chicken curry, and char kway teow.
   - Lau Pa Sat: This historic hawker center, also known as Telok Ayer Market, is famous for its satay, BBQ seafood, and diverse food stalls.

- Old Airport Road Food Centre: Located in a former airport terminal, it offers a wide array of local dishes, including carrot cake, oyster omelets, and Hokkien mee.
- Tiong Bahru Market: Situated in a charming neighborhood, it's popular for its local breakfast items like chwee kueh and lor mee.

3. Culinary Diversity:

Singapore's hawker centres are a testament to its multicultural society. You can savor Malay, Chinese, Indian, and other international cuisines all under one roof. From laksa and roti prata to dumplings and chili crab, the options are endless.

4. Affordable Dining:

Hawker centres are known for their affordability, making them accessible to locals and tourists alike. You can enjoy a delicious meal for a fraction of the cost you'd pay at a restaurant.

5. UNESCO Recognition:

In 2020, Singapore's hawker culture was inscribed on UNESCO's Representative List of the Intangible Cultural Heritage of Humanity. This recognition highlighted the importance of preserving and promoting hawker centers as a unique cultural heritage.

6. Cleanliness and Hygiene:
   Singapore takes food safety and hygiene seriously. All hawker centers are subject to strict regulations, ensuring that the food served is safe and of high quality.

7. Community Spaces:
   Hawker centers are not just about food; they serve as communal spaces where people from all walks of life come together to enjoy a meal, fostering a sense of unity and togetherness.

8. Modernization and Upgrades:
   Many hawker centers have undergone renovations and modernization to improve facilities, making them more comfortable for diners while retaining their traditional charm.

9. Challenges and Preservation:
   While hawker centers are an integral part of Singapore's culture, there are challenges, including the aging population of hawkers and the difficulty in passing down the culinary traditions to the next generation. The government and various initiatives are working on preserving this heritage.

In conclusion, Singapore's hawker centers offer a unique culinary experience, representing the country's multicultural diversity, affordability, and cultural heritage. They are a must-visit for anyone looking to explore the rich tapestry of flavors that Singapore has to offer.

- *Peranakan Cuisine*

Peranakan cuisine in Singapore is a fascinating and unique culinary tradition that reflects the vibrant cultural tapestry of the island nation. Peranakan culture, also known as Straits Chinese or Baba-Nyonya culture, is a blend of Chinese, Malay, and Indonesian influences, and their cuisine is a delicious reflection of this fusion.

1. Historical Background:
   Peranakan people are descendants of Chinese immigrants who married local Malays and Indonesians. This intermingling of cultures gave birth to a distinct Peranakan identity, complete with its own language (Baba Malay or Peranakan Malay), clothing, and, of course, cuisine. This cuisine has evolved over centuries and has played a significant role in shaping Singapore's diverse food scene.

2. Key Ingredients:

Peranakan cuisine combines a wide array of ingredients, making it exceptionally diverse and flavorful. Key ingredients include coconut milk, lemongrass, tamarind, galangal, candlenuts, and a variety of aromatic spices. These ingredients are skillfully combined to create rich, fragrant, and savory dishes.

3. Popular Dishes:
Some of the most iconic Peranakan dishes in Singapore include:
- Nyonya Laksa: A spicy coconut milk-based noodle soup.
- Ayam Buah Keluak: Chicken cooked with a unique nut that has a distinctive earthy flavour.
- Peranakan Popiah: A fresh spring roll filled with julienned vegetables, shrimp, and a sweet hoisin-based sauce.
- Rendang: A slow-cooked dry curry that is rich and flavorful.

4. Influence on Singaporean Cuisine:
Peranakan cuisine has made a significant impact on Singaporean food culture. Dishes like Laksa and Hainanese Chicken Rice have Peranakan roots. Many Singaporeans enjoy Peranakan dishes regularly, and restaurants serving this cuisine can be found across the island.

5. Cultural Significance:

Beyond its culinary excellence, Peranakan cuisine holds cultural significance. It is often associated with elaborate Peranakan weddings and festive celebrations. The vibrant and intricate Peranakan porcelain and batik textiles are also integral to this culture.

6. Restaurants and Hawker Centers:

Visitors to Singapore can savor authentic Peranakan cuisine at specialized Peranakan restaurants and stalls within hawker centers. Some renowned places include Blue Ginger, Candlenut, and the food stalls at Peranakan Place.

7. Modern Innovations:

While traditional Peranakan cuisine remains popular, modern chefs are putting innovative twists on classic recipes, offering a fusion of traditional flavors with contemporary presentation.

8. Preservation of Heritage:

Efforts have been made to preserve and promote Peranakan culture and cuisine. The Peranakan Museum in Singapore is dedicated to showcasing the rich history and traditions of the Peranakan people.

Peranakan cuisine in Singapore is a captivating fusion of cultures and flavors, offering a delightful culinary experience that reflects the diverse and dynamic nature of this island nation. Whether you're a local or a visitor, exploring the unique flavors of Peranakan cuisine is a must on your culinary journey through Singapore.

- *Seafood Specialties*

Singapore is renowned for its vibrant and diverse food scene, and its seafood specialties are no exception. With its strategic location by the sea and a rich cultural tapestry, Singapore offers a plethora of delectable seafood dishes that cater to a wide range of tastes and preferences. Here, we'll explore some of the must-try seafood specialties in Singapore:

1. Chilli Crab: Arguably Singapore's most famous seafood dish, chilli crab features mud crabs cooked in a savory, sweet, and slightly spicy tomato-based sauce. It's often enjoyed with deep-fried mantou buns for dipping and sopping up the luscious gravy.

2. Black Pepper Crab: Similar to chilli crab but with a spicier twist, black pepper crab is a beloved variation where the sauce is rich with the aroma of

black pepper. It offers a delightful balance of heat and flavour.

3. Hainanese Steamboat: This is a unique hotpot dish, where a pot of clear, fragrant chicken broth is used to cook fresh seafood like prawns, fish, and clams, along with an assortment of vegetables and tofu. Diners can also enjoy various dipping sauces.

4. Sambal Stingray: Stingray, marinated in a spicy sambal sauce made from chili, shrimp paste, and other ingredients, is wrapped in banana leaves and grilled. The result is a flavorful, smoky, and spicy delicacy that's a must-try for those who enjoy a kick of heat.

5. Salted Egg Crab: This dish features crab coated in a creamy salted egg yolk sauce, offering a delightful combination of rich and savory flavors. The buttery, golden sauce pairs perfectly with the succulent crab meat.

6. Cereal Prawns: A fusion of Chinese and Malay flavors, cereal prawns feature prawns coated in a fragrant mix of cereal, curry leaves, and chili. This dish is a crunchy and savory delight with a hint of spiciness.

7. Fish Head Curry: As the name suggests, this dish includes a whole fish head, often red snapper, cooked in a flavorful curry broth with vegetables. The curry is rich and aromatic, and it's usually served with rice or bread.

8. Oyster Omelette: A popular street food dish, the oyster omelette combines fresh oysters, eggs, and a starchy batter to create a crispy and gooey delicacy. It's often garnished with a tangy chilli sauce.

9. Laksa: While not exclusively a seafood dish, laksa is a fragrant noodle soup that can include prawns, fish, or squid. The soup is made with a rich coconut milk base and is flavoured with a blend of aromatic herbs and spices.

10. BBQ Sambal Stingray: This variation of sambal stingray involves grilling the fish with sambal sauce directly on banana leaves. The result is a smoky, spicy, and tender dish that's a favourite at hawker centres.

These are just a few examples of the seafood specialties you can savor in Singapore. Whether you prefer your seafood spicy, sweet, or savory, Singapore's culinary scene has something to satisfy every palate. Don't miss the opportunity to explore the diverse and delicious world of seafood when you visit the Lion City.

- *International Dining*

International dining in Singapore is a culinary journey like no other. The city-state's diverse and multicultural population has given rise to a vibrant food scene that offers an array of international cuisines. Here, you can savor the flavors of the world without leaving the island.

1. Chinese Cuisine: Singapore's Chinese cuisine is incredibly diverse. You can enjoy Cantonese, Szechuan, Teochew, and Hokkien dishes. Chinatown is a hub for delicious dim sum, Peking duck, and various regional specialties.

2. Malay Cuisine: Malay cuisine is a significant part of Singapore's culinary landscape. Dishes like nasi lemak (coconut rice with sambal), rendang (spicy beef stew), and laksa (spicy noodle soup) are popular choices.

3. Indian Cuisine: Little India is the go-to place for authentic Indian food. From dosa to biryani and tandoori dishes, the options are abundant. Singapore also boasts Michelin-starred Indian restaurants.

4. Peranakan Cuisine: Peranakan or Nyonya cuisine is a fusion of Chinese and Malay flavors. Dishes like laksa lemak and ayam buah keluak are unique to this culture and can be savored in specialty restaurants.

5. Japanese Cuisine: The Japanese food scene in Singapore is thriving, offering sushi, sashimi, ramen, and more. You'll find both high-end omakase dining and affordable sushi joints.

6. Korean Cuisine: The popularity of Korean culture has brought about a surge in Korean restaurants in Singapore. Try dishes like bibimbap, bulgogi, and of course, Korean barbecue.

7. Western Cuisine: From French fine dining to American-style burgers, Singapore has a wide range of Western options. High-end steakhouses, Italian trattorias, and contemporary European eateries can be found across the city.

8. Mediterranean Cuisine: Mediterranean restaurants offer delightful options like falafel, kebabs, and shawarma. Some places also provide stunning views of the Marina Bay Sands.

9. South-East Asian Cuisine: Beyond local Malay cuisine, you can explore the wider flavors of Southeast Asia. Thai, Vietnamese, Indonesian, and Filipino dishes can be found in dedicated restaurants.

10. African and Middle Eastern Cuisine: Singapore's diverse culinary scene extends to African and Middle Eastern flavors, with offerings like Moroccan tagine, Ethiopian injera, and Lebanese mezze.

11. Latin American Cuisine: You can find vibrant Latin American eateries serving up Mexican tacos, Brazilian churrasco, and Peruvian ceviche. These provide a fusion of bold and spicy flavors.

12. Vegetarian and Vegan Options: Singapore is increasingly accommodating to vegetarian and vegan diets. There are dedicated restaurants offering plant-based versions of international dishes.

13. Food Hawker Centers: While not exclusively international, hawker centers are a staple of Singapore's dining scene. They offer a variety of local and international dishes, making them great

places to sample a mix of flavours at affordable prices.

14. Fine Dining and Michelin-Starred Restaurants: Singapore boasts an impressive collection of fine dining establishments, including numerous Michelin-starred restaurants. These venues offer exquisite experiences in a range of international cuisines.

15. Food Festivals: Singapore hosts various food festivals and events throughout the year, such as the Singapore Food Festival and World Gourmet Summit, which celebrate international and local cuisines.

In summary, international dining in Singapore is a testament to the city's cosmopolitan nature. It's a gastronomic adventure where you can explore the world's flavors within a relatively small geographical area, making it a true food lover's paradise. Whether you're craving a particular cuisine or eager to try something new, Singapore's diverse culinary scene has something for everyone.

Chapter 7. Shopping Paradises

- *Orchard Road Shopping District*

Orchard Road is one of the most iconic and renowned shopping districts in Singapore. It is a vibrant, bustling street located in the heart of the city-state and is synonymous with high-end retail, entertainment, and luxury experiences. Here is an overview of Orchard Road:

1. Location and Accessibility:
   Orchard Road is situated in the Central Area of Singapore, running for approximately 2.2 kilometers. It is easily accessible via public transportation, with several MRT (Mass Rapid Transit) stations and bus stops located along the street. This accessibility makes it a popular destination for both locals and tourists.

2. Shopping Galore:
   Orchard Road is known for its numerous shopping malls, each offering a diverse range of retail experiences. Some of the most famous malls include ION Orchard, Ngee Ann City, Paragon, and Orchard Central. These malls house a plethora of high-end designer boutiques, electronics stores, department stores, and specialty shops. You can

find anything from the latest fashion trends to luxury watches and high-tech gadgets.

3. Luxury Brands and Boutiques:
   Many luxury brands have flagship stores along Orchard Road, making it a haven for fashion enthusiasts. High-end labels such as Louis Vuitton, Chanel, Gucci, and Prada are well-represented here. It's also a popular destination for those seeking fine jewelry and watches.

4. Dining and Entertainment:
   Orchard Road is not just about shopping; it's also a hub for dining and entertainment. Visitors can enjoy a wide array of culinary experiences, from street food stalls to Michelin-starred restaurants. The area comes alive at night with bars, clubs, and live music venues.

5. Cultural Attractions:
   Beyond shopping and dining, Orchard Road is home to some cultural landmarks. The Singapore Art Museum and the National Museum of Singapore are nearby. There's also the Istana, the official residence of the President of Singapore, which is occasionally open for public visits.

6. Festive Season:

Orchard Road is especially enchanting during the holiday season. The street is adorned with stunning Christmas decorations and lights, attracting tourists and locals alike. This annual spectacle includes various events, performances, and sales promotions.

7. Events and Promotions:

Throughout the year, Orchard Road hosts various events and promotions. Retailers often participate in the Great Singapore Sale, offering discounts and deals. The street also hosts fashion shows, art exhibitions, and food festivals.

8. Urban Greenery:

Orchard Road isn't just about concrete and commerce. The district has made efforts to incorporate green spaces and urban gardens. Dhoby Ghaut Green and the Istana Park provide pockets of greenery amidst the shopping frenzy.

9. History and Evolution:

Orchard Road has a rich history, having evolved from a nutmeg and fruit orchard in the early 19th century to the thriving shopping district it is today. Over the years, it has undergone significant development and expansion, becoming a symbol of modern Singapore.

10. Tourist Attraction:

Orchard Road is a major tourist attraction and is often one of the first places visitors explore when in Singapore. Its central location and the wide range of offerings make it an ideal destination for tourists looking to shop, dine, and experience the city's vibrant atmosphere.

In conclusion, Orchard Road is not just a shopping district; it's a symbol of Singapore's prosperity and modernity. It offers a comprehensive shopping and lifestyle experience, making it a must-visit destination for anyone looking to explore the dynamic and cosmopolitan side of Singapore.

- *Bugis Street Market*

Bugis Street Market is a vibrant and iconic street market located in the heart of Singapore. It has a rich history and is renowned for its unique shopping and dining experiences. Here's an overview of Bugis Street Market:

History:
Bugis Street Market has a fascinating history. Originally, it was a notorious red-light district in the 1950s and 1960s. However, the area underwent

significant urban redevelopment, and by the 1980s, it transformed into a bustling shopping destination.

Location:
Bugis Street Market is situated in the Bugis area, a historic and cultural district in Singapore. It's easily accessible by public transportation, making it a popular destination for both locals and tourists.

Shopping:
Bugis Street Market is renowned for its shopping options. The market boasts over 600 shops and stalls, offering a wide variety of goods. Shoppers can find everything from trendy clothing, accessories, and electronics to unique souvenirs and trinkets. It's a great place to pick up affordable fashion items and gifts.

Food and Dining:
The market is not just about shopping; it's also a culinary paradise. Numerous food stalls and eateries serve up a diverse range of local and international dishes. You can savor delicious Singaporean street food, including satay, laksa, and Hainanese chicken rice.

Night Market:

Bugis Street Market truly comes alive in the evening. It transforms into a night market with vibrant lights, creating a lively and atmospheric ambiance. This is when you can experience the market at its most energetic, with street performances and bustling crowds.

Bargaining:
While not as intense as in some other Southeast Asian markets, bargaining is still a common practice at Bugis Street. You can often negotiate prices, especially if you're buying multiple items from the same vendor.

Tourist-Friendly:
Bugis Street Market caters to tourists with English-speaking stallholders and clear signage. It's a great place to experience Singaporean culture and find unique souvenirs.

Entertainment:
Apart from shopping and dining, Bugis Street also hosts occasional events and performances, adding to the entertainment value of the market.

Accessibility:
The market is conveniently located near Bugis MRT station, which is a major transportation hub,

making it easily accessible from various parts of the city.

In summary, Bugis Street Market in Singapore is a must-visit destination for those looking for a lively and diverse shopping and dining experience. Its history, unique atmosphere, and convenient location make it an iconic part of Singapore's cultural and retail landscape.

- Unique Souvenirs

Singapore offers a wide array of unique souvenirs that capture the essence of this vibrant city-state. Whether you're a tourist looking for gifts or a local seeking to celebrate Singapore's rich culture, here are some ideas for unique souvenirs:

1. Peranakan-inspired Items: The Peranakan culture is an integral part of Singapore's heritage. You can find intricately designed Peranakan ceramics, clothing, and accessories. Items like "kebaya" tops, beaded slippers, or Nyonya porcelain make exceptional gifts.

2. Orchid-themed Products: Singapore's national flower is the orchid, and you can find a wide range of orchid-themed souvenirs. This includes

orchid-scented perfumes, orchid tea blends, and even preserved orchid jewelry.

3. Local Food Delights: Singapore is known for its diverse culinary scene. Packets of chili crab paste, Hainanese chicken rice mix, and laksa spice kits are perfect for food lovers. Alternatively, consider local snacks like kaya jam or bak kwa (barbecued pork slices).

4. Singaporean Tea: Singapore has a burgeoning tea culture, and you can find unique tea blends inspired by local flavors. Consider Pandan-infused tea or orchid tea to capture the essence of Singapore.

5. Traditional Clothing: The "Baju Kurung" or "Sarong" is traditional Malay attire. These garments come in various colors and patterns, making them a great souvenir for those interested in Singapore's multicultural society.

6. Art and Crafts: Singapore has a thriving arts and crafts scene. Look for locally crafted items like batik prints, wooden hand-carved masks, and contemporary artwork by Singaporean artists.

7. Merlion Merchandise: The Merlion is a symbol of Singapore, and you can find a wide range of

souvenirs featuring this iconic creature. These include keychains, figurines, and t-shirts.

8. Singaporean Jewelry: Local jewelers create exquisite pieces inspired by the city's skyline and natural beauty. Look for designs featuring the Marina Bay Sands, the Esplanade, or even the unique Supertree structures at Gardens by the Bay.

9. Traditional Toys and Games: Explore traditional games like "Five Stones" or "Kuti-Kuti" and toys such as handmade kites or spinning tops. These items offer a glimpse into Singapore's nostalgic past.

10. Customized and Personalized Souvenirs: Many stores in Singapore offer customization services. You can have your name or a special message engraved on items like chopsticks, keychains, and jewelry for a personal touch.

11. Vintage Collectibles: Antique shops and markets in Singapore offer unique vintage items. You might discover old Peranakan porcelain, vintage postcards, or even classic toys.

12. Cultural Books: Books about Singapore's culture, history, or cuisine can be a meaningful

souvenir. These can provide a deeper understanding of the place and its people.

13. Local Fabrics: Seek out traditional textiles like "Songket" or "Batik" fabric. These can be used for clothing, home decor, or craft projects.

14. Airlines' Memorabilia: Singapore Airlines is known for its quality service. Consider collecting unique items like amenity kits, playing cards, or model airplanes as mementos.

15. Plant and Herb-based Products: Singapore's lush botanical gardens make for excellent plant-inspired souvenirs. Look for items like natural soaps, scented candles, or essential oils made from local herbs and flora.

Remember to purchase your souvenirs from reputable stores or markets to ensure their authenticity and quality. Singapore's diverse culture and rich history offer a wealth of options for unique and memorable keepsakes that reflect the spirit of this dynamic city-state.

Chapter 8. Cultural Experiences

- *Museums and Art Galleries*

Museums and art galleries in Singapore are a vibrant and diverse part of the country's cultural landscape. Singapore, despite its small size, boasts an impressive array of institutions that showcase a wide range of artistic and historical treasures. Here's an overview of some of the most prominent museums and art galleries in the city-state:

1. National Gallery Singapore: Housed in two iconic heritage buildings, the former Supreme Court and City Hall, the National Gallery Singapore is home to the world's largest public collection of modern Southeast Asian art. It features works by artists from the region, including Singapore, Malaysia, Indonesia, and beyond. The museum also hosts international exhibitions and special programs.

2. ArtScience Museum: Located at Marina Bay Sands, the ArtScience Museum is a distinctive lotus-shaped building that combines art, science, culture, and technology. It regularly hosts immersive exhibitions that explore a wide range of topics, from art and innovation to the environment and social issues.

3. Singapore Art Museum (SAM): Focused on contemporary art, SAM is known for its diverse collection of modern and contemporary Southeast Asian art. It showcases various mediums, including paintings, sculptures, installations, and new media art. SAM also hosts the Singapore Biennale, a significant contemporary art event.

4. Peranakan Museum: This museum highlights the Peranakan culture, which is a unique blend of Chinese, Malay, and Indonesian influences. Visitors can explore the rich history and traditions of the Peranakan people through the museum's extensive collection of artifacts, textiles, jewelry, and ceramics.

5. Asian Civilisations Museum (ACM): ACM delves into the diverse cultures of Asia, including the regions of Southeast Asia, South Asia, East Asia, and West Asia. The museum features a remarkable collection of artifacts, religious art, and historical objects, offering a view of Asian heritage.

6. Lee Kong Chian Natural History Museum: For those interested in the natural world, this museum at the National University of Singapore is a must-visit. It houses an impressive collection of over a million specimens, including dinosaurs,

fossils, and an extensive array of Southeast Asian flora and fauna.

7. Red Dot Design Museum: Located in the vibrant Clarke Quay district, this museum celebrates the best in contemporary design. It showcases award-winning product designs from around the world, providing insights into the evolution of design and innovation.

8. National Museum of Singapore: The oldest museum in Singapore, the National Museum offers a look at the country's history and culture. It hosts a variety of exhibitions, interactive displays, and multimedia installations that bring the past to life.

9. Peranakan Tiles Gallery: This small yet charming museum is dedicated to preserving and showcasing the intricate and colorful Peranakan tiles that were once a prominent feature of Peranakan homes in Singapore. It offers a unique glimpse into this decorative art form.

10. Singapore Tyler Print Institute (STPI): This art space specializes in print and paper works, featuring collaborations with both local and international artists. It offers a unique perspective

on the art world, with a focus on innovative and experimental printmaking.

These museums and art galleries in Singapore cater to a wide range of interests, from contemporary art and natural history to cultural heritage and design. They contribute to Singapore's vibrant cultural scene, making the city a hub for art and knowledge. Whether you're a local resident or a visitor, exploring these institutions can be an enriching and educational experience.

- Traditional Festivals

Traditional festivals in Singapore are a vibrant reflection of the country's multicultural heritage. The city-state, known for its modernity and urban landscape, celebrates a diverse array of traditional festivals that showcase its rich cultural tapestry. Here's an overview of some of the most prominent traditional festivals in Singapore:

1. Chinese New Year: This is arguably the most significant traditional festival in Singapore, celebrated with great enthusiasm by the Chinese community. The city is adorned with vibrant decorations, and families come together for reunion dinners. The iconic Chingay Parade is a major

highlight, featuring dazzling floats and performances.

2. Hari Raya Puasa: Celebrated by the Malay Muslim community, Hari Raya Puasa marks the end of Ramadan. Festivities include communal prayers, visiting relatives, and enjoying traditional Malay dishes. The Geylang Serai district is famous for its elaborate decorations and bazaars during this festival.

3. Deepavali (Diwali): The Hindu festival of lights is celebrated with much fervor in the Little India district. Streets are adorned with colorful lights and intricate kolam (rice flour designs). Families light oil lamps and exchange gifts while visiting temples.

4. Mid-Autumn Festival: Also known as the Mooncake Festival, this Chinese festival revolves around the consumption of mooncakes and the lighting of lanterns. Chinatown is illuminated with lantern displays and various cultural performances. Mooncakes are exchanged as a symbol of unity and togetherness.

5. Thaipusam: A Hindu festival celebrated with a grand procession, Thaipusam is an extraordinary spectacle. Devotees pierce their bodies with skewers

and carry elaborate kavadis (metal frames) as acts of penance and devotion. The procession takes place at the Sri Srinivasa Perumal Temple.

6. Vesak Day: A Buddhist festival commemorating the birth, enlightenment, and passing of Buddha. Devotees visit temples to make offerings and participate in candlelit processions. The Buddha Tooth Relic Temple and Museum in Chinatown is a significant location for these celebrations.

7. Chingay Parade: While not exactly a traditional festival, the Chingay Parade is an integral part of Singapore's cultural calendar. It's a colorful and extravagant event with multicultural performances, featuring vibrant costumes and massive floats.

8. Pongal: A Tamil harvest festival, Pongal is celebrated in Little India, typically in January. It involves cooking a special dish of newly harvested rice, and decorative kolam designs are drawn on the streets.

9. Hungry Ghost Festival: This Taoist and Buddhist festival is dedicated to ancestral spirits. It is believed that the gates of the afterlife open during this month, and offerings are made to appease and

honor the spirits. You can observe traditional performances in some areas.

10. Good Friday: Celebrated by the Christian community, Good Friday is a significant religious holiday. Churches hold special services, and the Christian community gathers for solemn processions and prayers.

Singapore's government actively promotes the celebration of these traditional festivals as a means of preserving cultural heritage and fostering intercultural understanding. These festivals not only offer a glimpse into the diverse cultures that coexist in Singapore but also provide opportunities for residents and visitors to participate in and appreciate the customs, rituals, and cuisines that make this city-state so unique.

- Theatres and Performances

Singapore has a vibrant and thriving arts and culture scene, with a rich history of theatrical performances and a commitment to promoting the performing arts. The city-state boasts a diverse range of theatres, performance venues, and cultural events that cater to both locals and tourists. In this overview, we'll explore the history, key venues, and notable performances in Singapore's theatrical landscape.

Historical Context:
Singapore's love for the performing arts can be traced back to its colonial past when British settlers introduced Western theater traditions. However, it was in the 20th century, after gaining independence in 1965, that the nation began to nurture its own unique theater culture. The government's support for the arts, including substantial funding and infrastructure development, has played a significant role in shaping the theater scene.

Key Theatres and Performance Venues:
1. Esplanade - Theatres on the Bay: Often referred to as "The Durian" due to its unique spiky architecture, the Esplanade is an iconic performing arts center. It hosts a wide range of events, from classical concerts to contemporary theater, and is a focal point for Singapore's artistic community.

2. Victoria Theatre and Concert Hall: This historic venue, dating back to 1862, has been meticulously restored and is a hub for classical music, dance, and theater performances. Its neoclassical architecture adds to the charm of the cultural events hosted here.

3. Drama Centre Singapore: Located at the National Library Building, the Drama Centre serves as a platform for local and international theater productions. It also nurtures emerging talent through its drama education programs.

4. SOTA Concert Hall: Part of the School of the Arts (SOTA), this modern concert hall hosts a variety of performances, showcasing the talents of young artists and students.

5. The Warehouse: Theatre of the Arts: An intimate black box theater located in a converted warehouse, this venue offers a more experimental and edgy space for contemporary performances.

Notable Performances:
Singapore has witnessed a diverse array of performances over the years. Some notable productions and annual events include:

1. Singapore International Festival of Arts (SIFA): SIFA is an annual event that celebrates both local and international performances. It features a mix of theater, dance, music, and visual arts.

2. Shakespeare in the Park: Held at Fort Canning Park, this outdoor theater series brings Shakespearean classics to life under the starry Singaporean night.

3. Wild Rice Productions: Known for its groundbreaking and socially relevant performances, Wild Rice is a theater company that often stages productions that challenge the status quo.

4. Cultural Festivals: Singapore's multicultural society also ensures that a diverse range of cultural festivals and performances, from Chinese opera to Indian dance, are celebrated throughout the year.

5. Local and Emerging Artists: Singapore supports local talents and emerging artists through platforms like the M1 Singapore Fringe Festival and the Emerging Directors' Showcase, providing opportunities for fresh and innovative works.

In conclusion, Singapore's theaters and performances offer a dynamic mix of cultural experiences, bridging the gap between tradition and innovation. With state-of-the-art venues and a commitment to artistic expression, the city-state continues to be a thriving hub for the performing arts, attracting both local and international talent.

Whether you're a theater enthusiast or a casual spectator, Singapore has something to offer for everyone in its ever-evolving theatrical landscape.

Chapter 9. Outdoor Adventures

- *Singapore Zoo*

The Singapore Zoo, located in Singapore, is one of the most renowned and well-maintained zoological parks in the world. Officially known as the Mandai Zoological Gardens, it spans 28 hectares and is home to over 2,800 animals representing more than 300 species, making it a must-visit attraction for both locals and tourists.

Here are some key aspects of the Singapore Zoo:

1. History: The zoo was first opened in 1973 and has since undergone numerous expansions and renovations. It has consistently focused on creating naturalistic habitats for its animals.

2. Open Concept: One of the zoo's most unique features is its open concept. Instead of traditional enclosures with bars and cages, many animals are housed in spacious, landscaped exhibits with hidden barriers like moats and glass walls, providing visitors with the illusion of being closer to the animals in a more natural environment.

3. Animal Exhibits: The Singapore Zoo offers a wide variety of animal exhibits, from the Fragile Forest,

where you can walk among free-flying birds and animals, to the Frozen Tundra, featuring polar bears and raccoon dogs. There's also the Primate Kingdom, which houses a diverse range of primates, and the Reptile Garden for reptile enthusiasts.

4. Conservation Efforts: The zoo is heavily involved in conservation efforts and breeding programs, particularly for endangered species. They have successfully bred animals like the white rhinoceros and the orangutan.

5. Night Safari: Adjacent to the zoo is the Night Safari, another popular attraction. It is the world's first nocturnal zoo and allows visitors to see a variety of animals that are more active at night, such as tigers, lions, and various nocturnal creatures.

6. River Safari: Located nearby, the River Safari is yet another part of the Mandai Zoological Gardens. It focuses on aquatic and riverine animals, featuring giant pandas, manatees, and an impressive Amazon Flooded Forest exhibit.

7. Education and Outreach: The zoo is dedicated to educating visitors about wildlife conservation and animal behavior. It conducts various educational

programs, including zoo camps and wildlife tours, and has a strong commitment to spreading awareness about endangered species and environmental issues.

8. Dining and Amenities: The Singapore Zoo offers a range of dining options and amenities, including various eateries and picnic spots for visitors. There are also trams and guided tours available for those who want to explore the zoo more comfortably.

9. Accessibility: The zoo is easily accessible by public transportation and is located in the Mandai area of Singapore, surrounded by lush greenery. It provides a unique opportunity to experience nature and wildlife in the midst of a bustling city.

In summary, the Singapore Zoo is not just a tourist attraction but a center for wildlife conservation, education, and an exemplary model of creating habitats that prioritize the well-being of the animals. Its commitment to maintaining high standards of animal care and providing a memorable and educational experience for visitors has made it a world-class destination for animal lovers and conservation enthusiasts.

- *Night Safari*

The Night Safari in Singapore is a world-renowned nocturnal zoo and one of the city-state's most unique and popular attractions. Opened in 1994, it is the first of its kind globally, dedicated to showcasing the diverse wildlife that comes alive after the sun sets. Here's an overview of the Night Safari:

1. Location: The Night Safari is located within the Singapore Zoo premises in Mandai, in the northern part of Singapore. It covers an expansive area of 35 hectares and is home to over 2,500 animals from various regions around the world.

2. Nocturnal Experience: The main feature of the Night Safari is the opportunity to observe animals in a nighttime environment that mimics their natural habitats. It's designed to replicate the conditions of a tropical rainforest, with cleverly concealed lighting that allows visitors to see the animals without disturbing their activities.

3. Animal Collection: The Night Safari is home to a diverse range of animals, including tigers, lions, leopards, elephants, giraffes, rhinoceroses, and various species of deer. It's particularly well-known

for its impressive collection of exotic and endangered species.

4. Creatures of the Night Show: One of the highlights of the Night Safari is the "Creatures of the Night Show." It's a live presentation that showcases the natural behaviors and abilities of nocturnal creatures like owls, civets, and hyenas.

5. Tram Safari: The Night Safari offers both walking trails and tram rides through the park. The tram ride is a popular option as it takes visitors on a guided tour through the park, allowing them to see animals up close while being under the watchful care of experienced guides.

6. Walking Trails: For a more immersive experience, visitors can explore walking trails that lead them through different zones, including the Fishing Cat Trail, Leopard Trail, and Wallaby Trail, each focusing on a specific group of animals.

7. Conservation Efforts: The Night Safari is actively involved in conservation and research efforts, including breeding programs for endangered species. It plays a crucial role in the protection and preservation of these animals and their habitats.

8. Dining and Entertainment: The Night Safari offers various dining options, including local and international cuisine. There are also cultural performances and entertainment shows to enjoy in the park.

9. Accessibility: The Night Safari is easily accessible by public transportation, and many hotels in Singapore offer tour packages that include a visit to the Night Safari. It's open daily, except on certain public holidays.

10. Awards and Recognitions: The Night Safari has received numerous awards and accolades over the years, including being recognized as one of the best nocturnal zoos in the world.

In summary, the Night Safari in Singapore is a unique and captivating experience that allows visitors to appreciate the wonders of the animal kingdom under the shroud of darkness. It blends education, conservation, and entertainment, making it an exceptional destination for nature enthusiasts and families alike.

- *Pulau Ubin*

Pulau Ubin is a small island located in the northeastern part of Singapore. Known for its rustic charm and natural beauty, Pulau Ubin stands in stark contrast to the urban landscape of mainland Singapore. Here is an overview of Pulau Ubin:

1. Geography and Location:
   Pulau Ubin is situated just off the northeastern coast of Singapore and is part of the Ubin planning area. The island covers an area of approximately 10.2 square kilometers, making it one of the few remaining undeveloped areas in Singapore.

2. History:
   The name "Pulau Ubin" translates to "Granite Island" in Malay, referring to the island's history of granite quarrying. In the early 20th century, the island was a major source of granite used in the construction of many iconic buildings in Singapore. The quarries have since been abandoned and have filled with rainwater, creating picturesque lakes.

3. Natural Beauty:
   Pulau Ubin is known for its lush greenery and diverse flora and fauna. It's a haven for nature enthusiasts and birdwatchers. The island boasts numerous walking and cycling trails, allowing visitors to explore its rich biodiversity.

4. Kampongs (Villages):

There are a few kampongs (traditional villages) on Pulau Ubin, where some residents still live in traditional wooden houses. These villages provide a glimpse into Singapore's rural past and are popular with tourists.

5. Chek Jawa Wetlands:

One of the island's most famous attractions is Chek Jawa, a wetland ecosystem on the eastern side of Pulau Ubin. It's a unique and ecologically diverse area with tidal flats, mangroves, and seagrass lagoons.

6. Outdoor Activities:

Pulau Ubin offers a range of outdoor activities, including hiking, mountain biking, camping, and kayaking. There are rental shops on the island where visitors can rent bicycles and kayaks.

7. Ketam Mountain Bike Park:

For mountain biking enthusiasts, Pulau Ubin offers the Ketam Mountain Bike Park, a network of trails suitable for riders of different skill levels.

8. Conservation Efforts:

The Singapore government and various environmental groups have made efforts to conserve Pulau Ubin's natural environment. The island is part of the Ubin-Khatib Important Bird Area, recognized for its importance to the conservation of bird species.

9. Transportation:
   The only way to reach Pulau Ubin is by boat. A short bumboat ride from Changi Point Ferry Terminal connects the mainland to the island. Once on the island, visitors can explore on foot or rent bicycles.

10. Cultural and Historical Significance:
   Beyond its natural beauty, Pulau Ubin also holds cultural and historical significance for Singapore. It's a living link to Singapore's past, showcasing a simpler and more traditional way of life.

11. Development and Conservation Balance:
   Over the years, there have been discussions and debates about preserving Pulau Ubin's natural beauty while accommodating development. Efforts have been made to strike a balance, with some areas being conserved and others designated for low-impact development.

In conclusion, Pulau Ubin is a remarkable enclave of nature and history in the heart of Singapore. Its pristine environment and cultural significance make it a unique destination for both local and international visitors seeking to escape the city's hustle and experience a more tranquil and rustic side of Singapore.

- *East Coast Park*

East Coast Park is a popular and iconic recreational area located in Singapore, known for its stunning coastal views and wide array of activities. Stretching along the eastern coast of Singapore, it covers approximately 185 hectares of reclaimed land, making it one of the city-state's largest and most beloved parks.

History:
East Coast Park's history can be traced back to the 1970s when the Singapore government initiated a massive land reclamation project along the eastern shoreline. The aim was to create a park that would cater to the recreational needs of the growing population. Over the years, the park has undergone numerous enhancements, making it the vibrant and diverse destination it is today.

Activities:
East Coast Park offers a plethora of activities that cater to visitors of all ages and interests. These activities include:

1. Cycling: The park boasts a dedicated cycling track that stretches throughout its length, making it a perfect spot for cyclists to enjoy a scenic ride along the coast.

2. Beach and Water Sports: Visitors can engage in a variety of water sports, such as swimming, kayaking, windsurfing, and even cable skiing at the nearby lagoon. There are also designated areas for picnicking and barbecues.

3. MDining: The park is home to numerous restaurants, hawker centers, and cafes. This makes it a great place for families and friends to enjoy a delicious meal with a beautiful seaside backdrop.

4. Fishing: Fishing enthusiasts can take advantage of the designated fishing areas, which offer an opportunity to catch various species of fish.

5. Skating and Skateboarding: The park features a skate park, providing a space for skateboarders and inline skaters to practice their skills.

6. Outdoor Fitness Areas: There are outdoor fitness stations scattered throughout the park, allowing

people to exercise while enjoying the fresh sea breeze.

7. Nature Trails: For those who prefer a more leisurely experience, there are nature trails that allow visitors to explore the local flora and fauna.

Events and Festivals:
East Coast Park is also a hub for various events and festivals throughout the year. Events such as beach parties, outdoor movie screenings, and sports tournaments are frequently held here, adding to the vibrancy of the park.

Accessibility:
The park is easily accessible, with multiple car parks and public transport options, including bus services and a nearby MRT station, making it convenient for residents and tourists alike.

Conclusion:
East Coast Park is a quintessential Singaporean destination, offering a wide range of recreational activities, dining options, and natural beauty. Whether you're looking for a day of family fun, outdoor adventures, or simply a place to relax by the sea, East Coast Park has something for everyone. It's a testament to Singapore's

commitment to providing accessible and enjoyable outdoor spaces for its citizens and visitors.

Chapter 10. Nightlife and Entertainment

- *Clarke Quay*

Clarke Quay is a vibrant and historic riverside quay in Singapore that has become a popular destination for both locals and tourists. Located along the Singapore River, Clarke Quay is known for its lively atmosphere, diverse entertainment options, and a rich history. Here is an overview of Clarke Quay:

History:
- Clarke Quay is named after Sir Andrew Clarke, who was the second Governor of the Straits Settlements in the late 19th century. It was originally a commercial hub, handling goods and cargo from boats and bumboats along the river.

Entertainment and Nightlife:
- Today, Clarke Quay is primarily known for its vibrant nightlife and entertainment options. The area comes alive at night, with a plethora of bars, restaurants, and nightclubs. It's a popular spot for those looking to enjoy the city's nightlife.

Dining Options:
- Clarke Quay offers a diverse range of dining experiences, from local hawker stalls serving traditional Singaporean cuisine to upscale

international restaurants. You can savor a wide variety of dishes, from chili crab to sushi.

Shopping:
- Clarke Quay is not just about dining and entertainment; it's also a shopping hub. There are numerous boutique shops and retail outlets, offering everything from fashion to souvenirs.

Architecture and Scenic Views:
- The area has retained its historical architecture, with colorful, colonial-style buildings lining the riverside. This adds to the charm of the place. The picturesque views of the river and the skyline create a beautiful backdrop for dining and leisure activities.

Cultural and Art Events:
- Clarke Quay often hosts cultural and art events, such as live music performances, art exhibitions, and cultural festivals. These events add to the cultural vibrancy of the area.

Boat Tours:
- Singapore River boat tours can be accessed from Clarke Quay, allowing visitors to explore the city from a unique perspective. These tours offer insights into the city's history and landmarks.

Connectivity:
- Clarke Quay is well-connected by public transport, making it easy for visitors to access from various parts of Singapore. The nearest MRT station is the Clarke Quay station on the North East Line.

Family-Friendly Activities:
- While known for its nightlife, Clarke Quay also offers family-friendly activities. These include the G-Max Reverse Bungy, which offers an adrenaline-pumping experience, and the Singapore River Cruise, which is suitable for all ages.

In summary, Clarke Quay is a multifaceted destination in Singapore that seamlessly blends history, entertainment, dining, shopping, and cultural experiences. Whether you're looking for a lively night out, a taste of Singaporean cuisine, or a place to enjoy scenic river views, Clarke Quay has something for everyone. It remains a must-visit spot for those exploring the rich tapestry of Singapore's attractions.

- Club Street

Club Street is a well-known and vibrant area in Singapore, situated in the heart of the Chinatown district. This historic street has evolved into a popular destination, characterised by its eclectic mix of restaurants, bars, and boutique shops. Here's an overview of Club Street in Singapore:

1. Historical Significance: Club Street has a rich history dating back to the 19th century when it was named after the Chinese Weekly Entertainment Club that once occupied the area. The street has preserved some of its historical architecture and charm, making it a unique and attractive location.

2. Dining and Cuisine: One of the main draws of Club Street is its diverse culinary scene. It is home to a wide range of restaurants, serving cuisines from around the world. Visitors can savor everything from authentic Chinese and Peranakan dishes to Italian, French, and modern fusion cuisine. This makes Club Street a food lover's paradise.

3. Nightlife: As the sun sets, Club Street comes alive with a bustling nightlife scene. The street is lined with bars and pubs, offering an array of craft beers, cocktails, and live music. It's a popular spot for both locals and tourists to unwind after a long day.

4. Boutique Shops: In addition to the culinary delights and nightlife, Club Street also boasts

several boutique shops. You can find unique fashion boutiques, art galleries, and specialty stores selling handcrafted goods. It's a great place for shopping enthusiasts looking for something out of the ordinary.

5. Art and Culture: Club Street occasionally hosts art events and exhibitions, contributing to the local art and culture scene. It's not uncommon to find art galleries showcasing works from local and international artists.

6. Street Markets: The adjacent Ann Siang Hill area hosts periodic street markets. These markets feature a variety of products, from handmade crafts to vintage items, adding an extra layer of charm to the neighborhood.

7. Architectural Beauty: The shophouses along Club Street and the surrounding area are an architectural delight. These well-preserved buildings reflect the heritage of the city, with their distinctive facades, colorful shutters, and intricate detailing.

8. Accessibility: Club Street is conveniently located in the central business district, making it easily accessible via public transportation, including the

Chinatown MRT station. This accessibility makes it a popular spot for both locals and tourists.

9. Community Events: Club Street often hosts community events, such as street parties and food festivals. These events provide opportunities for residents and visitors to come together, enjoy good food, and celebrate the vibrant atmosphere of the street.

10. Tourist Attraction: Due to its unique character, Club Street has become a must-visit destination for tourists looking to experience the cultural diversity and dynamic culinary scene that Singapore has to offer.

In summary, Club Street in Singapore is a dynamic and culturally rich destination that combines history, culinary excellence, nightlife, and a vibrant community. It stands as a testament to Singapore's ability to blend its heritage with modernity, creating a unique and engaging atmosphere that appeals to a wide range of visitors.

- Rooftop Bars

Rooftop bars in Singapore offer a unique and luxurious experience, combining stunning cityscape views with delicious drinks and a vibrant atmosphere. Singapore's skyline is renowned for its iconic architecture and beautifully lit skyscrapers, making it an ideal setting for rooftop bars. Here's an overview of the rooftop bar scene in Singapore:

1. Marina Bay Sands SkyPark: This iconic rooftop features an infinity pool and a breathtaking 360-degree view of the city. While it's mainly for hotel guests, you can visit the observation deck for a fee.

2. CÉ LA VI: Located atop the Marina Bay Sands, CÉ LA VI is a stylish rooftop bar offering handcrafted cocktails, a modern Asian menu, and unparalleled vistas of the city.

3. Lantern at The Fullerton Bay Hotel: Overlooking Marina Bay, this rooftop bar provides a chic ambiance, making it a popular spot for both tourists and locals.

4. 1-Altitude: Situated on the 63rd floor of One Raffles Place, 1-Altitude is the highest rooftop bar in Singapore. It offers stunning 360-degree panoramic views and a high-energy nightlife experience.

5. Artemis Grill: This Mediterranean-inspired rooftop bar is located in the CBD and boasts a lush

garden terrace and delicious food. It's known for its sustainability practices.

6. The Rooftop at Screening Room: Found in the heart of Chinatown, this rooftop bar provides a cozy setting, making it a great spot for intimate gatherings.

7. Mr Stork: Set in Andaz Singapore, Mr Stork features a teepee-inspired setting, surrounded by lush greenery, and offers a relaxed vibe that's perfect for unwinding.

8. LeVel33: It's the world's highest urban craft brewery, located at Marina Bay Financial Centre. Guests can enjoy freshly brewed craft beers and spectacular views.

9. Smoke & Mirrors: Situated at the National Gallery Singapore, this rooftop bar has a sophisticated atmosphere, creative cocktails, and a view of the Padang and Marina Bay Sands.

10. 1927 Rooftop Bar: Tucked away in the historic SO Sofitel Singapore, this bar combines vintage charm with modern elegance, offering guests a refined experience.

11. Southbridge: This rooftop bar on Boat Quay offers a splendid view of the Singapore River and a diverse menu of oysters, cocktails, and wines.

12. OUE Social Kitchen: This rooftop destination in the heart of the CBD offers a unique "live kitchen" concept where you can watch chefs prepare your food as you enjoy the view.

13. Ce La Vi SkyBar: Located at the top of a heritage building in the heart of the CBD, this bar is known for its stunning views and vibrant nightlife scene.

14. The Warehouse Hotel Rooftop: Situated along the Singapore River, this rooftop offers a mix of history and modernity, making it a popular choice for both tourists and locals.

15. Empire: Located in the National Museum of Singapore, Empire offers a combination of culture, history, and modern luxury with its rooftop bar experience.

Keep in mind that dress codes, reservations, and age restrictions may vary from one rooftop bar to another. It's a good idea to check in advance and make reservations if necessary, especially during peak times. Rooftop bars in Singapore provide an excellent opportunity to enjoy the city's skyline, unwind, and socialize in a glamorous setting.

Chapter 11. Family-Friendly Activities

- *Universal Studios Singapore*

Universal Studios Singapore is a world-renowned theme park located on the resort island of Sentosa in Singapore. Opened in 2010, it is part of the larger Resorts World Sentosa complex and is known for its thrilling rides, immersive attractions, and a wide array of entertainment options. Here is an overview of Universal Studios Singapore:

1. Park Layout: Universal Studios Singapore is divided into seven themed zones, each offering a unique experience:
   - Hollywood: The entrance to the park and reminiscent of the Golden Age of Hollywood.
   - New York: Resembles the iconic cityscape of the Big Apple.
   - Sci-Fi City: A futuristic zone featuring attractions like the Transformers ride.
   - Ancient Egypt: Transporting visitors back to the time of pharaohs and mummies.
   - The Lost World: Themed around the Jurassic Park franchise with exciting dinosaur-themed attractions.
   - Far Far Away: Inspired by the Shrek films and fairy tales.

- Madagascar: Based on DreamWorks' Madagascar franchise.

2. Rides and Attractions: Universal Studios Singapore is famous for its exhilarating rides and immersive attractions. Some of the must-try rides include:
   - Battlestar Galactica: A dueling roller coaster.
   - Transformers: The Ride: A 3D simulator experience.
   - Revenge of the Mummy: A high-speed indoor roller coaster.
   - Jurassic Park Rapids Adventure: A water ride with dinosaurs.
   - Shrek 4-D Adventure: An interactive show.
   - Puss in Boots' Giant Journey: A family-friendly roller coaster.

3. Entertainment: In addition to rides, the park offers live shows and entertainment featuring beloved characters from Universal Studios movies. You can catch parades, street performances, and character meet-and-greets throughout the day.

4. Dining and Shopping: Universal Studios Singapore provides a variety of dining options, from fast food to fine dining. The park also offers themed

merchandise shops where you can buy souvenirs related to your favorite movies and characters.

5. Halloween Horror Nights: Every year, the park hosts a Halloween event where the entire park is transformed into a haunted playground with terrifying mazes, scare zones, and special themed shows.

6. Special Events: Universal Studios Singapore often hosts special events and festivals, such as Lunar New Year celebrations, Christmas events, and more, making it a year-round destination.

7. Accessibility: The park is easily accessible via a monorail from mainland Singapore. It's a popular attraction for tourists and locals alike.

8. Tickets: Universal Studios Singapore offers various ticket options, including one-day passes and annual passes for frequent visitors. It's advisable to check the official website for up-to-date pricing and availability.

In summary, Universal Studios Singapore offers a diverse range of experiences, from thrilling rides and immersive attractions to live entertainment and special events. It's a fantastic destination for visitors of all ages, whether you're a fan of Universal's iconic movies or just looking for an exciting day out in Singapore.

- S.E.A. Aquarium

The S.E.A. Aquarium, located in Resorts World Sentosa on Sentosa Island in Singapore, is one of the world's largest aquariums and a popular tourist attraction. Here's an overview of this remarkable aquatic exhibit:

1. Size and Scope:
  - The S.E.A. Aquarium covers a vast area of 12,000 square meters, making it one of the largest aquariums globally.
  - It's home to more than 100,000 marine animals from over 1,000 species.

2. Open Ocean Habitat:
  - One of the main highlights of the S.E.A. Aquarium is the Open Ocean habitat, which features a colossal viewing panel measuring 36 meters wide and 8.3 meters tall.
  - Visitors can watch awe-inspiring species like manta rays, sharks, and various schools of fish swimming in a habitat that mimics the open ocean.

3. Themed Zones:

- The aquarium is divided into different themed zones, each representing a specific marine ecosystem. These include the Strait of Karimata & Java Sea, Shark Seas, and the Persian Gulf & Arabian Sea.

4. Conservation and Education:
   - The S.E.A. Aquarium places a strong emphasis on marine conservation and education. Visitors can learn about the importance of protecting the oceans and its inhabitants.
   - The facility participates in various conservation and research efforts to protect endangered marine species.

5. Exhibits and Species:
   - In addition to the Open Ocean habitat, the S.E.A. Aquarium showcases a diverse array of marine life, including seahorses, jellyfish, lionfish, and many types of corals.
   - The exhibits are designed to be both visually stunning and informative.

6. Interactive Experiences:
   - The aquarium offers several interactive experiences for visitors, including touch pools where you can interact with sea stars and sea cucumbers.

- There are also behind-the-scenes tours and programs for a deeper understanding of marine life.

7. Events and Shows:
 - The S.E.A. Aquarium hosts various events and shows throughout the year. These might include diver feeding sessions and educational talks.

8. Accessibility:
 - The S.E.A. Aquarium is easily accessible from Singapore's city center, as it's located on Sentosa Island. Visitors can use various transportation options, including a monorail and cable car.

9. Timings and Tickets:
 - It's advisable to check the official website for the most up-to-date information regarding opening hours, ticket prices, and any special promotions.

10. Overall Experience:
 - The S.E.A. Aquarium offers a captivating and educational experience for visitors of all ages, making it a must-visit attraction for those interested in marine life and conservation.

Remember that details such as opening hours, ticket prices, and specific exhibits may change over time, so it's a good idea to check the official website or contact the aquarium directly for the most current information before planning your visit.

- Kid-Friendly Parks

Singapore offers a plethora of kid-friendly parks and outdoor spaces that cater to the needs and interests of children of all ages. These parks provide opportunities for play, exploration, and learning in a safe and beautiful environment. Here's an overview of some of the most popular kid-friendly parks in Singapore:

1. Gardens by the Bay:
   - Located in the heart of the city, Gardens by the Bay features the Cloud Forest and Flower Dome conservatories. Children can explore lush greenery, fascinating flora, and stunning architecture.
   - The Children's Garden within the park offers a water play area, treehouses, and interactive installations for kids to enjoy.

2. East Coast Park:
   - This beachside park is a favorite among families. It has extensive cycling and rollerblading paths, barbecue areas, and large open spaces for picnics.
   - Children can enjoy the Marine Cove playground, which includes a water play area and a massive climbing structure.

3. Jurong Bird Park:
   - Home to thousands of birds from around the world, the Jurong Bird Park provides a unique educational experience for kids.
   - Children can enjoy bird shows, feeding sessions, and even have the opportunity to interact with some of the feathered residents.

4. Singapore Zoo:
   - The Singapore Zoo offers a world-class wildlife experience. Kids can explore various animal exhibits, such as the Fragile Forest and the Rainforest Kidzworld water park.
   - The Night Safari and River Safari, located nearby, provide additional wildlife encounters.

5. HortPark:
   - HortPark is known as a gardening hub and a great place for kids to connect with nature. The park features themed gardens, a butterfly garden, and a gardening resource center.
   - Children can participate in educational workshops and explore the lush surroundings.

6. Jacob Ballas Children's Garden:
   - This dedicated children's garden within the Singapore Botanic Gardens is designed to educate

and entertain kids. It includes a suspension bridge, treehouses, and water play areas.
- The garden is a fantastic place for kids to learn about plants and nature in a hands-on way.

7. Bishan-Ang Mo Kio Park:
- This park is famous for its waterway and river plains. Children can explore water play areas and adventure playgrounds.
- The park also offers picturesque walking and cycling trails for the whole family.

8. Pasir Ris Park:
- Located in the eastern part of Singapore, Pasir Ris Park is perfect for outdoor activities. It has a large playground, bicycle rentals, and a wide beach area.
- Families can enjoy picnics, fishing, and water sports in this scenic park.

9. Wild Wild Wet:
- If your kids love water adventures, Wild Wild Wet is a water park in Pasir Ris offering thrilling water rides, wave pools, and lazy rivers.
- It's a perfect place for a fun-filled day of splashing and sliding.

10. Universal Studios Singapore:

- While not a traditional park, Universal Studios Singapore is a theme park on Sentosa Island, where kids can immerse themselves in their favorite movie worlds.
- It offers a range of rides, shows, and character meet-and-greets for children of all ages.

These kid-friendly parks in Singapore offer a wide range of experiences, from nature exploration and educational opportunities to water fun and thrilling adventures. Families visiting Singapore will find plenty of options to keep children entertained while creating lasting memories.

Chapter 12. Practical Tips

- *Safety Considerations*

Safety considerations in Singapore are of paramount importance, as the city-state has a reputation for being one of the safest places in the world. This is achieved through a combination of strict regulations, effective law enforcement, and a proactive approach to ensuring the safety and well-being of its residents and visitors. Below, we will explore several key aspects of safety considerations in Singapore:

1. Public Safety:
   - Low Crime Rate: Singapore boasts one of the lowest crime rates globally. The government's strong stance on law enforcement and strict penalties for criminal activities act as a strong deterrent.
   - Surveillance: The city is equipped with extensive surveillance systems, including security cameras, to monitor public spaces and deter potential wrongdoers.

2. Road Safety:
   - Traffic Rules: Singapore enforces strict traffic rules and regulations. Speed limits and traffic laws

are rigorously maintained, contributing to road safety.

  - Strict Penalties: Heavy fines and penalties for traffic violations help deter reckless driving.

3. Fire Safety:

  - Mandatory Fire Drills: Building owners and managers are required to conduct regular fire drills to ensure residents and employees are well-prepared in case of emergencies.

  - Stringent Building Codes: Singapore has strict building codes and regulations to minimize fire hazards.

4. Healthcare and Medical Safety:

  - World-Class Healthcare: Singapore offers high-quality healthcare services with well-trained medical professionals.

  - Strict Health Regulations: The government maintains stringent health regulations, ensuring cleanliness and hygiene in healthcare facilities.

5. Environmental Safety:

  - Clean Environment: Singapore places great emphasis on environmental safety, ensuring clean air and water.

- Green Initiatives: The city-state has numerous green initiatives, such as tree planting and waste recycling, to maintain a sustainable environment.

6. Emergency Services:
   - Quick Response: Singapore's emergency services, including the police and medical teams, are known for their swift response times.
   - Well-Prepared: Singapore conducts regular emergency response exercises to ensure preparedness for any situation.

7. Natural Disaster Preparedness:
   - Hurricane and Flood Protection: Singapore invests heavily in infrastructure to protect against natural disasters, such as hurricanes and flooding.
   - Early Warning Systems: The country has effective early warning systems to alert residents about potential natural disasters.

8. Cybersecurity:
   - Robust Cybersecurity: In the digital age, Singapore places great importance on cybersecurity, with measures to protect critical infrastructure and data from cyber threats.

9. Food Safety:

- Strict Regulations: Singapore's food safety regulations are rigorous, ensuring that food products are safe for consumption.
- Regular Inspections: Authorities conduct routine inspections of food establishments to maintain high standards.

10. Workplace Safety:
- Occupational Safety and Health: Singapore has strict regulations to ensure the safety and well-being of employees in the workplace.
- Training and Education: Employers are required to provide training and education on workplace safety.

In conclusion, Singapore's commitment to safety considerations is a cornerstone of its success as a city-state. It has earned a global reputation for being a safe place to live, work, and visit. The government's proactive approach, strict regulations, and investment in infrastructure and technology all contribute to the high level of safety enjoyed by its residents and visitors.

- Local Etiquette

Local etiquette in Singapore is rooted in a diverse cultural heritage, predominantly influenced by Chinese, Malay, Indian, and Western customs.

Understanding and respecting these etiquettes is crucial when visiting or living in Singapore. Here is an overview of local etiquette in Singapore:

1. Greetings:
  - A common greeting is a handshake, but it is often light.
  - Address people with courtesy titles (Mr., Mrs., or Miss) and their surname unless invited to use their first name.

2. Respect for Elders:
  - Show respect to older individuals with a polite greeting and addressing them as "Uncle" or "Auntie."
  - Give up your seat on public transport to the elderly.

3. Gift-Giving:
  - When giving gifts, use both hands or the right hand, and it's polite to refuse a gift a few times before accepting it.
  - Gifts should be wrapped nicely.

4. Dining Etiquette:
  - Remove your shoes before entering someone's home.

- Wait to be seated and don't start eating until the host or eldest person does.
- Use utensils to eat, especially in formal settings. Eating with your hands is acceptable in some situations but not at formal occasions.
- It's customary to bring a small gift, like fruit or sweets, when visiting someone's home.
- Do not point your feet at people, as it's considered disrespectful.

5. Chopsticks:
- Do not stick your chopsticks upright in a bowl of rice, as it resembles incense offerings at funerals.

6. Punctuality:
- Arriving on time is highly valued, so make an effort to be punctual for appointments and meetings.

7. Public Behaviour:
- Chewing gum is banned in Singapore, so avoid bringing or chewing gum in public.
- Littering is illegal and heavily fined, so dispose of trash properly.

8. Dress Code:
- Dress modestly in public places and temples.

- Avoid wearing revealing clothing outside of the beach areas.

9. Language and Gestures:
   - English is one of the official languages, but knowing a few words in Malay, Chinese, or Tamil can be appreciated.
   - Use polite language and avoid raising your voice in public.

10. Tipping:
    - Tipping is not a common practice in Singapore. A service charge is usually included in the bill at restaurants.

11. Religious Sites:
    - When visiting temples or mosques, dress modestly and remove your shoes before entering.

12. Queuing:
    - Singaporeans take queuing seriously, so wait your turn in an orderly fashion.

13. Traffic and Transportation:
    - Always obey traffic rules and stand in designated areas while waiting for public transport.

14. Public Displays of Affection:

- Public displays of affection should be kept to a minimum, as they are generally not encouraged in public.

15. Cultural Sensitivity:
   - Be mindful of Singapore's diverse population, and avoid discussing sensitive topics like race, religion, or politics.

16. Environmental Respect:
   - Singapore places a strong emphasis on cleanliness and environmental conservation, so do your part by disposing of trash responsibly and conserving resources.

By adhering to these etiquettes, you will show respect for the local customs and culture in Singapore, making your experience more enjoyable and harmonious while visiting or living in the city-state.

Chapter 13. Itinerary Suggestions

- 3 Days in Singapore: Exploring the Highlights

Exploring the highlights of Singapore in three days is an exciting adventure that allows you to experience the diverse culture, stunning architecture, delicious cuisine, and natural beauty of this vibrant city-state. Here's an itinerary for a 3-day trip to Singapore:

Day 1: Discovering the Cultural Heart
- Morning: Start your day at Chinatown, where you can explore colorful streets, visit historic temples like the Buddha Tooth Relic Temple, and savor a traditional breakfast at a local hawker center.
- Late Morning: Head to Little India, known for its vibrant markets, fragrant spices, and stunning temples like Sri Veeramakaliamman Temple.
- Lunch: Enjoy a diverse Indian cuisine at one of the many local eateries.
- Afternoon: Visit the National Museum of Singapore to delve into the city's rich history. Then, take a stroll along Orchard Road, Singapore's shopping haven.
- Evening: Explore Clarke Quay, known for its bustling nightlife. You can dine at a riverside

restaurant, take a river cruise, or visit the iconic Merlion Park for a stunning view of the city skyline.

Day 2: Modern Marvels and Nature
- Morning: Start your day at Gardens by the Bay, an architectural wonder featuring the Supertree Grove and the stunning Flower Dome and Cloud Forest.
- Late Morning: Visit the nearby Marina Bay Sands and take in panoramic views from the iconic SkyPark.
- Lunch: Savor lunch at one of the many dining options within the Marina Bay Sands complex.
- Afternoon: Explore Sentosa Island, where you can visit Universal Studios, Adventure Cove Waterpark, or relax on the beautiful beaches.
- Evening: Return to the city and have dinner in the vibrant Arab Street area. Don't forget to visit the Sultan Mosque.

Day 3: Nature, Heritage, and Local Delights
- Morning: Spend your morning at the Singapore Botanic Gardens, a UNESCO World Heritage site, and enjoy a leisurely walk among lush greenery.
- Late Morning: Head to Tiong Bahru, a trendy neighborhood known for its charming cafes and unique boutiques.
- Lunch: Try the local delicacy Hainanese chicken rice at one of the famed hawker stalls.

- Afternoon: Explore the historic district of Kampong Glam, home to the impressive Sultan Mosque and numerous art galleries.
- Evening: End your trip with a visit to the futuristic Jewel Changi Airport, where you can experience the stunning indoor waterfall and enjoy a last meal before departure.

Singapore offers a rich tapestry of cultural experiences, modern marvels, and natural beauty. This 3-day itinerary will help you make the most of your visit and leave you with lasting memories of this captivating city.

- 5 Days in Singapore: Immersive Cultural Experience

Spending 5 days in Singapore can provide an immersive cultural experience that combines the city-state's rich history, diverse heritage, and contemporary dynamism. Here's an itinerary for an enriching cultural journey:

Day 1: Discovering Chinatown
- Start your cultural exploration in Chinatown, a vibrant district filled with historic shophouses and temples.

- Visit Sri Mariamman Temple, the oldest Hindu temple in Singapore, and explore its intricate architecture.
- Stroll through Chinatown Heritage Centre to learn about the early Chinese immigrants' lives.
- Enjoy a delicious Chinese meal at a local hawker center like Chinatown Complex.

Day 2: Exploring Little India
- Begin your day in Little India, where you can experience the sights, sounds, and flavors of India.
- Explore the colorful Sri Veeramakaliamman Temple and Sri Srinivasa Perumal Temple.
- Visit Mustafa Centre, a 24-hour shopping mall offering an eclectic range of products.
- Savor authentic Indian cuisine at eateries like Komala Vilas or The Banana Leaf Apolo.

Day 3: A Taste of Peranakan Culture
- Dive into Peranakan culture by heading to the Joo Chiat-Katong neighborhood.
- Explore the colorful Peranakan shophouses and visit the Peranakan Museum.
- Savor traditional Peranakan cuisine at a local restaurant like True Blue Cuisine.
- Take a guided tour of the Katong Antique House to learn more about the culture.

Day 4: Modern and Traditional Singapore
- Start your day with a visit to Gardens by the Bay, where the Supertree Grove and Cloud Forest provide a blend of nature and innovation.
- Head to the Civic District and explore historical landmarks like the National Museum and Singapore Art Museum.
- Visit the impressive Sultan Mosque in Kampong Glam, where you can explore the rich Islamic heritage.
- For a modern twist, experience the futuristic wonders of Marina Bay Sands.

Day 5: A Journey through History
- Explore Sentosa Island, known for its historical sites like Fort Siloso and the Surrender Chambers.
- Immerse yourself in Singapore's maritime heritage at the Maritime Experiential Museum.
- In the afternoon, visit the Asian Civilisations Museum to understand the diverse cultures that have shaped Singapore.
- End your cultural journey with a trip to Orchard Road for shopping and to experience the city's modern, cosmopolitan side.

Throughout your 5-day cultural experience in Singapore, you'll encounter a fusion of traditions and innovations, which makes the city a unique and captivating destination. Don't forget to sample local dishes at hawker centers, engage with the friendly locals, and explore the lesser-known corners of the city to truly appreciate its cultural richness.

Printed in Great Britain
by Amazon

30876955R30086